John Morris

Luther at Wartburg castle

A reformation story of 1521

John Morris

Luther at Wartburg castle
A reformation story of 1521

ISBN/EAN: 9783337127152

Printed in Europe, USA, Canada, Australia, Japan

Cover: Foto ©ninafisch / pixelio.de

More available books at **www.hansebooks.com**

LUTHER

AT

WARTBURG CASTLE.

A Reformation Story of 1521.

BY

THE AUTHOR OF "FIFTY YEARS IN THE LUTHERAN MINISTRY."

PHILADELPHIA:
LUTHERAN PUBLICATION SOCIETY,
1882.

Copyright, 1882.

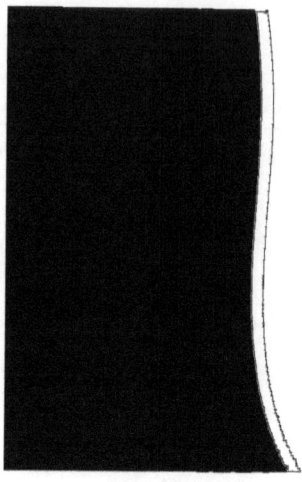

WESTCOTT & THOMSON,
Stereotypers and Electrotypers, Philada.

PREFACE.

MANY of the facts recorded in this little book are familiar to readers of Reformation history, but they have never before been brought together in a continuous narrative in the English language. They have been collected from numerous books concerning Luther, and the well-authenticated facts alone have been incorporated in this volume.

JOHN G. MORRIS.

CONTENTS.

ALBERT, count of Mansfeld, 30.
Albert, archbishop of Mayence, 67.
Aleander, 19.
Alphonzo Valdez, 20.
Altenstein castle, 32.
Amsdorf, 25.

BLACK BEAR INN, 94.
Bulla Cœna Domini, 75.
Burkard von Hund, 23, 24.

CAPTURE of Luther, 9, 32.
Carlstadt, 81.
Caspar Sturm, imperial herald, 24.
Charles V., 13.
Charles, edict of, 17.
Count von Meiningen, 35.
Count von Henneberg, 43.

D'AUBIGNÉ, 57.

EDICT of Charles V., 17.
Edict, false, date of, 19.

Edict, opinions about, 20.
Elector Frederick, 83.
Elizabeth, canonized, 10.
Elizabeth, her tomb, 10.
Emser, 66.
Erasmus, 88.
Erfurt, students of, 31, 94.

FRANCIS I., 22.
Frankfort, 25.
Frederick the Wise, 22, 34.
Friedheim, 27.

GABRIEL DIDYMUS, 81.
George, duke of Saxony, 22, 26, 41.

HALLER, 11.
Hans von Berlepsch, 23, 34.
Hermann, 1, 9.
Huss, John, 25.
Hutten, Ulrich, 93.

JACOB, Luther's brother, 26, 31.
Jerome Schurf, 25.
John Drach, 31.
John Oswald, 83.
John Petzenstein, 25.
John Suaven, 25.

KESSLER, Swiss student, 94.
Kotzebue, murder of, 11.
Kranach, the artist, 26, 27.
Krato, Meilius, abbot, 29.

CONTENTS.

LATORMUS, theologian, 65.
Leipzig, battle of, 10.
Lewis the Leaper, 9.
Linden tree at Mora, 3.
Luther, capture of, 9.
    at Worms, 14.
    room at Wartburg, 13.
    various letters, 26, 27, etc.
    courage of, 15.
    sale of his writings, 21.
    progress of his cause, 21.
    beech tree, 35.
    fountain, 34.
    portrait of, 38.
    age when captured, 32.
    despondency, 45, 47, 52.
    industry, 80.
    temptations, 53.
    the Swiss students, 85.
    return to Wittenberg, 73.

MARBURG, 10.
Marcolfus, 39.
Matthesius, 51.
Melanchthon, 93 (*passim*).
Melchior Lotther, Luther's printer, **79.**
Michelet, 56.
Minnesingers, 10.
Mora, 31.
Myconius, 55.

OPPENHEIM, 24.

PARIS, theological faculty, 66.
Peter the Great, 13.

SAFE-CONDUCT, 16.
Sand, Kotzebue's murderer, 11.
Schmaltz, 11.
Spalatin, 23, 28.

THURINGIA, 9.

WARTBURG CASTLE, 9, 14, 37, 47.
    celebration at, 10.
    Luther's treatment at, 14.
    Squire George, 52.
    hunting expedition, 52.
    legend of the inkstand, 56.
    Luther's temptations at, 53.
    Luther's studies at, 60.
    writings at, 61, 62, 64, 65, 67, 68, 71, 72, 75, 76, 77.
Wittenberg, 25.
Worms, 13.

ZWICKAU PROPHETS, 81.

LUTHER AT WARTBURG CASTLE.

CHAPTER I.

WARTBURG CASTLE.

THE capture of Luther by order of the elector Frederick, after the departure of the Reformer from Worms, where he had been summoned to answer for his alleged heresies, and his detention in the castle of Wartburg from May 4, 1521, to March 2, 1522, have imparted an unspeakably great historical interest to this mediæval fortress. It is situated on a hill nearly fourteen hundred feet high, a few miles distant from the town of Eisenach, in the territory of Saxe-Weimar. It was erected in the year 1070 by Lewis the Leaper, and was for two hundred years the residence of the landgraves of Thuringia. In 1264 that country came into the possession of Henry the Illustrious, who made the Wartburg his residence until his death, and his successors continued to occupy it until 1406. After this time the castle underwent many changes. It was inhabited by various noble families, of whom history gives very unsatisfactory and unreliable information; but this much is certain—that it has been the scene of some events of great historical importance.

It was the theatre of the poetic contests of the Minnesingers in the year 1200 under Herman I., and was also rendered memorable in those early days as the residence of the holy Elizabeth, the wife of Herman, who, for her distinguished virtues, was canonized shortly after death. Various miracles are ascribed to her, and the steps leading to her tomb, in Marburg, are worn hollow by the knees of thousands of pilgrims who for nearly seven hundred years have visited her final resting-place to be healed of their various maladies by touching her magnificently-jewelled coffin.

The Wartburg was the scene of another stirring event within the present century. On October 18, 1817, the anniversary of the battle of Leipzig was celebrated by more than five hundred students and professors from twelve of the universities of Germany. It was also announced as a commemoration of the third century of the Reformation. Social festivities and religious services were held in the Hall of the Knights, and speeches which were considered seditious and revolutionary by the government spies, were delivered. At night some indiscreet students made a bonfire of the writings of such men as Kotzebue, Schmaltz, Haller, Kamptz, and others who were suspected of being inimical to the popular rights of Germany. They also cast into the flames a corporal's staff, in imitation of the burning of the pope's bull by Luther. They performed many other objectionable acts which created great excitement throughout all Europe, and which became subject of grave consideration by several governments, who apprehended that these students aimed at introducing republicanism into Germany. The excitement culminated in the murder of Kotzebue by a student named Sand in March, 1819, which created a political ferment on the whole continent.

For hundreds of years, Wartburg Castle had been suffered to fall into decay, but within the present century the grand duke of Weimar, to whom it belongs, has expended large sums in the restoration of it to its original size and imposing proportions. For many years it was nothing more than a magnificent ruin of the Middle Ages, but now the broken walls have been rebuilt, the shattered apartments have been renewed and refurnished according to the ancient pattern. The gates, corridors, archways, galleries, court, armory, bastions, chapel, towers, and all that constitutes the majesty of a fortress of that remote period, have been renovated, excepting the apartments occupied by Luther, and it is at present the ornament and the pride of the territory.

Thousands of visitors every year ascend the hill on which the castle is perched for the purpose of seeing the small and dingy apartment which is immortalized as the dwelling-place and study of Luther, during his seven months' captivity. There is no doubt that this is the veritable room in which the mighty Reformer wrote and prayed and wept.

"Die Stätte die ein guter Mensch betrat
Ist eingeweiht; nach hundert Jahren klingt
Sein Wort und seine That dem Enkel wieder."*

It is a poorly-furnished room, containing nothing more than an old earthen stove, an awkwardly-constructed table, a worm-eaten chair—which was probably not Luther's original—an antique bookcase held together by large round-headed nails and heavy hinges, a few defaced portraits and the vertebra of a whale, which is given out as Luther's footstool. A relic undoubtedly genuine, covered with a small pane of glass, is seen above the door, and it is nothing more than the word "PETER" coarsely written in chalk, which tradition tells us is the original writing of Peter the Great when he visited the Wartburg. The marks of the legend of Luther hurling his inkstand at the devil in the shape of a great fly which had annoyed him are still visible on the wall, but they are regularly freshened up for the benefit of all credulous

---

* The place once trodden by a righteous man
Is sacred; centuries may revolve,
And still the echo of his voice and deeds
Is heard.

visitors. It seems almost a pity to break the charm of this little story, but it is proper to state that Luther's letters—which are the rich source of information concerning all events happening to him at this period—do not mention it, and it doubtless arose from the fact that in the activity of his imagination he attributed everything unfavorable in temporal or spiritual affairs to the direct personal agency of the devil, just as he blamed the envious Satan for revealing the secret of his presence at the Wartburg.

The small glass panes of the window which looks out upon the Thuringian Forest are glazed with strips of sheet-lead, and it opens in the middle like a double door.

The occasion of Luther's sojourn at the Wartburg will appear from the following narrative.

He had been summoned from Wartburg to a meeting at Worms by the emperor Charles V. to defend himself against the charge of heresy and insubordination. His friends vehemently urged him not to appear, but he persisted, and nothing could intimidate him. The boldness he displayed was heroic to the highest degree, and the whole world has heard of these exhibitions of Christian fortitude with unspeakable admiration. "The papists," said he on observing the anxiety of his friends, "do not wish me to go to Worms, but they are longing for my condemnation and death. It matters not. Pray not for me, but for the triumph of the word of God. Before my blood has grown cold thousands of men in the world will have become responsible for having shed it. The most holy adversary of Christ, the father, the master, the generalissimo of murderers, insists on its being shed. So be it: let God's will be done. Christ will give me his Spirit to overcome those ministers of error. I despise them during my life; I shall triumph over them by my death. They are very busy at Worms in devising measures which shall compel me to retract, and this shall be my retraction: I said formerly that the pope is Christ's vicar; now I assert that he is our Lord's adversary and the devil's apostle."

Luther appeared before the august assembly, composed of the emperor, numerous princes of the realm, many high ecclesiastical dignitaries and people of every rank and degree, the majority of whom were bitterly opposed to his doctrine and person. He valiantly maintained his cause before this distinguished assembly, and stoutly refused to recant a single point unless proved erroneous from the Scriptures. After discussing the different doctrines with the most learned theologians of the Romish Church and compelling the admiration of his worst enemies by his dexterity and fluency in debate, the profundity of his learning, the meekness of his spirit and his lion-hearted courage, he was permitted to leave Worms under the protection of "a safe-conduct"* from the emperor, although some of his enemies of high ecclesiastical and civil rank recommended several measures for ridding the Church of this pestilent heretic. This "safe-conduct," or government protection, was limited to a certain number of days, at the expiration of which the bearer could not claim any rights based upon it; but he could be seized

---

*That which gives a safe passage; either a convoy or guard to protect a person in an enemy's country or in a foreign country, or a writing, a pass or warrant of security given to a person to enable him to travel with safety.—*Webster.*

and punished like any other alleged malefactor.

Charles, instigated by some powerful enemies of Luther, issued an edict on May 26, 1521, authorizing any one to seize and deliver him up after the lapse of the time granted by the passport. A few sentences will give an idea of this edict:

"We have therefore dismissed from our presence this Luther, whom all pious and sensible men deem a madman or one possessed of the devil; and we enjoin that on the expiration of his safe-conduct immediate recourse be had to effectual measures to check his furious rage.

"For this reason, under pain of incurring the penalty due to the crime of high treason, we forbid you to harbor the said Luther after the appointed term shall expire, to conceal him, to give him food or drink, or to furnish him, by word or by deed, publicly or secretly, with any kind of succor whatever. We enjoin you, moreover, to seize this devil Martin Luther clothed in human form and in the garb of a monk, or cause him to be seized, wherever you may find him, to bring him before us without any delay, or to keep him in safe custody until you have learned from us in what manner you are to act toward him, and have received the reward due to your labors in so holy a work.

"As for his adherents, you will apprehend them, confine them and confiscate their property.

"As for his writings, if the best nutriment becomes the detestation of all men as soon as one drop of poison is mingled with it, how much more ought such books, which contain a deadly poison for the soul, to be not only rejected, but destroyed? You will therefore burn them or utterly destroy them in any other manner."

This imperial mandate sounded more like a papal bull than an act of the empire. In it Luther is execrated as an incorrigible heretic accursed of God and the pope. All his sins are painted in the blackest colors; the contents of his books are set forth as genuine doctrines of devils. They are represented as inciting war and sedition, robbery and murder; as dissolving all the bonds of the State and of the Church and annihilating the entire

Christian system. The unheard-of insolence, as it was called, with which he rages against all the decrees of the pope and of councils, the holy sacraments, sacerdotal discipline and church order, are depicted in the most offensive language. He is represented as denying all legal and moral obligation, leading a lawless life and indulging in unbridled licentiousness. We need not be surprised at this edict when we know that it was written by the papal legate Aleander, one of Luther's most furious enemies.

One interesting fact in the history of this edict must not be overlooked. It was not promulgated until the 26th of May, at which time the Diet had been dissolved and most of the members had left Worms; but, to give it the appearance of an act of the Diet, it was purposely dated May 8 and had not received the sanction of many members. The few men who adopted it did not meet in the hall of the imperial assembly, but the emperor convened them in his own private apartments, where the act was consummated; and, to make it appear to have been unanimously adopted, a spurious date was attached to it.

Such was the proclamation issued by the emperor, and all men were commanded to observe it. It placed Luther and his friends in a fearful predicament. There were thousands who were ready to execute it, for they thirsted for his blood and would have made a merit of putting him to death. But the Lord preserved him from the machinations of the wicked, for Luther had not yet accomplished the work for which he was raised up. All the adherents of Rome burst into a shout of triumph. The victory was achieved. The outlawed monk could easily be apprehended, and dealt with accordingly. Others, more farseeing, entertained different views. "In my opinion," said Alphonso Valdez, a Spaniard at the court of Charles, "it is not the end, but the beginning; for I find that the minds of the Germans are much excited against the papal chair." He was right. The cause had taken such deep root in the Church and in the people that, even should Luther be put to death, the Reformation would not perish with him. Everybody was aware of the danger to which he was exposed, but still some discriminating men believed that the revolution had taken too firm a hold upon the hearts of thousands to be put back, even though the leader of it should be put out of the way. Some of the most influential states of the empire had openly expressed their disapprobation of the abominable oppressions of the pope and his allies. They spoke with reverence of the heroic Luther, and had themselves abolished some of the abuses of the Church. In many towns the people had espoused the new doctrine, and no one dared to publish the edict of Worms, "for fear of the people." At many places the Lutheran party was so strong that the Romanists were compelled to keep quiet. Even in Worms, Luther's writings were sold in the streets before the emperor had left the city.

In the condition of things then existing, it could be foreseen that the edict would not produce important results. Some of the states did not conceal their admiration of Luther's bearing at the Diet; to others this religious controversy was a matter of too much indifference to allow the edict to be seriously carried into effect in their territories. Besides these, for a long time the majority of the states had established it as a principle to employ every method to weaken the influence of the papal assumptions relating to German affairs. The emperor himself was at that time involved in a war with Francis I. of France, and he had neither time nor power to execute the wishes of the Roman court. It was only in the states of Duke George of Saxony and of the elector of Brandenburg in which any unfavorable results for the Lutheran party were to be apprehended.

Frederick the Wise, elector of Saxony, the sovereign of Luther, was highly delighted with his courageous conduct at the Diet; but he knew well enough that he would incur the odium and opposition of the emperor and his party if he openly resisted the edict and in defiance of it protected the outlawed Reformer. He conceived a plan by which he could shield him from the wrath of his enemies and grant him rest for a season from his exhausting labors.

If he could secrete him for a while from public observation and let the report go forth that Luther was murdered, the excitement would subside and the general apprehension be quieted. It is said by some that even the emperor himself was privy to this scheme, but the report is not authentic. Frederick had Luther apprehended on his return from the Diet, and he was secretly conveyed to Wartburg Castle.

The elector was much too conscientious to expose himself to the dilemma of knowing where Luther was concealed and thus appearing to maintain a stand of opposition to his sovereign, and hence he left the execution of the design to his court-preacher and private secretary, Spalatin. He selected the Wartburg as the most desirable asylum, and employed the bold and stalwart castellan Hans von Berlepsch to carry out the plan in its details. The latter took into his confidence a nobleman of the vicinity, Burkard von Hund, and also employed other subordinates. It was only the day before Luther left Worms that Spalatin succeeded in gaining his consent to the capture, but without informing him where it was to occur or to what place he was to be conducted. Perhaps they were afraid that his candor or want of caution or abhorrence of all duplicity might lead him to betray the secret.

CHAPTER II.

THE CAPTURE.

IT was Friday, April 26, 1521, when Luther left Worms on his return home. After he had given his farewell benediction to his friends, many of whom had visited him on the eve of his departure, and having partaken of a frugal meal, he left the place at 10 A. M., accompanied by some who had determined to go with him all the way to Wittenberg, and by others who could proceed only a short distance. Casper Sturm, the imperial herald, in his official costume, followed him after a few hours, and overtook him at Oppenheim and acted as his protector under direct orders of the emperor. Charles was too well aware of the opinion of the princes and of the states, as well as of the people, and, besides, he was too conscientious himself, to allow Luther to be exposed to the violence of his enemies.

Instead of yielding to the murderous importunity of those who urged him not to observe the rights of the safe-conduct to the heretic, but to treat him as Huss was treated at Constance one hundred years before, he despatched one of his own trusty henchmen to guard him against violence.

It must be recorded to the credit of the emperor that to some princes at Worms who advised him to execute Luther he replied: "No. As Luther came here under the imperial protection and safe-conduct, we will not consent that any harm shall befall him; for if fidelity to one's promises were driven out of all the world besides, it should still be found in an emperor."

In the same vehicle which the magistracy of Wittenberg had furnished to convey Luther to Worms, and in which he now entered on his homeward journey, there were seated with him, when they started, his friends Nicolas von Amsdorf, Justus Jonas, Jerome Schurf —who was his legal adviser at the Diet—John Suaven—a Pomeranian nobleman who was a student at Wittenberg—and John Petzensteiner, a brother of some order, who, according to its rules, was obliged to accompany him to Worms. Luther's own brother Jacob joined him subsequently.

On April 28 they arrived at Frankfort, where he received many tokens of regard from his friends and patrons. From this place he wrote a letter to his friend Lucas Kranach in Wittenberg, informing him of the proceedings at Worms, in which he says: "Nothing more was done than, 'Did you write these books?'—'Yes.'—'Will you recant them?'—'No!'—'Then begone.' O we blind Germans! how like children we act, and so miserably allow ourselves to be fooled by the Romanists!"

He had been informed of his intended capture, and submitted to it with hesitation; but he remembered how the servant of the Lord, Obadiah, the chamberlain of King Ahab, took a hundred prophets and hid them by fifty in a cave, and fed them with bread and water to protect them against the vengeance of the ungodly queen Jezebel (1 Kings xviii. 4), and how the disciples took Paul by night and let him down by the wall in a basket (Acts ix. 25), and how the wise men were warned of God in a dream to avoid the snares laid for them by Herod (Matt. ii. 12). In the letter to Kranach he takes leave of him and alludes to his contemplated apprehension, and continues: "I bless you and commend you to God. I will consent to be concealed, but I do not know where it is to be; and, although I would rather have suffered death from tyrants, especially from the infuriate Duke George, yet I must not disregard the counsel of good men. For a brief season we must keep silent and suffer. 'For a little while ye shall not see me, but in a little while ye shall see me.' Thus speaks Christ (John xvi. 15). I hope that may be your experience; but God's will be done in this, as in all other things, on earth as it is in heaven."

The imperial edict against Luther was not yet publicly proclaimed, but the report of his heroic conduct at Worms had spread abroad as if by a winged messenger. His journey homeward was like a triumphal procession, for many who were certain that he would fall a sacrifice to priestly tyranny and hate now hailed him and his friends with rapture.

On the same day they arrived at Friedheim. Here they rested for a short period, during which Luther wrote a long Latin letter to the emperor, and another of similar import, in German, to those electors, princes and states of the Holy Roman Empire who were assembled in Worms. In both he vindicated his conduct at the Diet in moderate and dignified language, and promised, although he could not succeed in having his writings examined by competent judges in Worms, that he would appear before such judges anywhere and recant if his facts and arguments were refuted by the Holy Scriptures. For the security of the safe-conduct he again expressed his thanks; he had expressed his gratitude personally to the emperor before he had left Worms. On the following day he despatched both letters by the hands of the imperial herald to Spalatin, who was still at that place, to be by him delivered to the parties addressed. The herald was thus dismissed, and this was an important step, for he might be in the way of carrying out the design; and, besides, his presence was no longer necessary, for they were now approaching the dominions of the landgrave Philip of Hessia, who had given Luther a safe-conduct through his territory.

It is probable that he wrote these letters at the instigation of the elector, for in an enclosed note to Spalatin he says: " Here you have the letters which you desired."

From Friedheim the journey was continued through the territory of the landgrave of Hessia, passing by Grünberg, Hersfeld and Berka, until, on the evening of May 1, they reached Eisenach, near which they were met by a crowd of citizens, who escorted them into the town.

At Hersfeld, Luther was received with great respect by the abbot Krato Meilius. "The abbot," says he, "sent his chancellor and chamberlain a whole mile to meet me, and he himself received me with numerous horsemen at his castle and conducted me into the village. At the gate the magistrates awaited me; in the monastery I was sumptuously entertained, and had a most comfortable chamber and a soft bed. They compelled me to preach next morning at five o'clock, although I resisted this appeal, for I was afraid it might be the occasion of detriment to the abbot, and they would also say that I had broken my promise, as they had forbidden me to preach during my journey. Yet I did not keep silence, and did not consent that the word of the Lord should be bound. The next day the abbot furnished me with an escort as far as the forest, and ordered his chancellor to provide another meal for us all at Berka. I also preached at Eisenach. True, the pastor of the church protested against it through a notary and witnesses, but afterward apologized by saying that he did it only from necessity and fear of his superiors."

Thus Luther reports his tour to Spalatin. In another letter from Eisenach to Count Albert of Mansfeld he says: "They enjoined it upon me not to preach or write during my journey. I said, 'I will do everything that is agreeable to His Imperial Majesty, and yet I will leave God's word unbound.' Thus I departed, and am now in Eisenach. Mark well, they will accuse me of having forfeited my safe-conduct, for I have preached at Hersfeld and Eisenach, and they interpret the prohibitory language very strictly."

At Eisenach he was received by a crowd

of the citizens, as at Hersfeld; and, whilst he was calmly sleeping in "his own dear city," there was on the same night a tumultuous uproar of his youthful admirers, principally students, in Erfurt, occasioned by a fierce attack of the deacon of one of the churches, from the steps of the high altar, upon Dr. Johann Drach, a professor in the university, who was an adherent of the new doctrine.

At Eisenach his travelling associates, excepting Amsdorf, separated from him. Most probably he was here joined by his brother Jacob, who accompanied him, on May 3, to Möra—"the Nazareth of Germany"—the former residence of his parents, where his grandmother and his uncle Heinz Luther, and many other relatives, still lived.

He here preached under a linden tree, for the chapel was much too small to contain the crowd that streamed from all quarters to hear their distinguished relative; so that he could justly write: "I travelled through the forest to see my relatives, who are so numerous that they occupy nearly the whole neighborhood." This linden is said to have stood before the original Luther house as late as fifty years ago, and was reckoned to be five hundred or six hundred years old.

Luther was at this time thirty-eight years old. He was of medium size, robustly built, but so reduced by cares and hard study that when he was approached near, all his bones could be counted. In his countenance, which also gave evidence of night-vigils and mental conflicts, there glowed two fiery eyes whose piercing glance it was hard to endure. At this time he still wore the cowl of the monk.

The next day he pursued his journey with his two companions to Waltershausen. The way leads near to the castle of Altenstein and passes through the Thuringian Forest. Near the castle, in a narrow defile, the vehicle was suddenly stopped by five masked and armed horsemen. One of them attacked the postilion and hurled him to the earth; another seized Amsdorf and held him firmly. He begged for mercy, but Luther, understanding the whole affair, pacified his alarmed fellow-travellers by saying, "*Confide, amici nostri!*" ("Be of good courage; they are our friends.")

The other three horsemen with feigned violence dragged Luther from the carriage, threw a military cloak over him and ordered him to mount a horse, before provided.

According to another account, when Luther was violently dragged out of the wagon he uttered the words, "Hell, hast thou conquered?" This exclamation might be interpreted as though he assumed he was apprehended by enemies in a region where the doctrines of Rome were still tenaciously held, and that he was not aware of what was to occur; but it can be easily reconciled to his consoling words to Amsdorf, inasmuch as he knew the diabolical plans with which he was persecuted, and which rendered his concealment from the world necessary. Without these wicked and malicious spirits his concealment would not have been necessary; and he may have meant this when he made the exclamation.

Luther's brother, Jacob, fled in alarm and concealed himself in the forest. The two who had Amsdorf and the coachman in custody now left them alone. All five leaped to their saddles and hurried away in a rapid gallop with their prisoner. The brother of the order had fled, without so much as a parting salutation, to Waltershausen.*

The coachman, alarmed to the highest degree, soon recovered sufficient consciousness to resume his place, and, taking Amsdorf into the wagon, drove at a rapid speed to Wittenberg. All along the road, in every village and to every one they met, they reported the violent abduction of Luther, and the alarming news soon spread over all the country around. The people were astonished and indignant, and the exclamation was everywhere heard, "Luther has fallen into the hands of his enemies."

The captors of Luther in the mean time proceeded in the direction of Wartburg, where they arrived at eleven o'clock at night. The whole transaction was performed, under the direction of the elector Frederick, by the castellan of Wartburg, Hans von Berlepsch, and his friend Burkhard Hund von Wenkheim.

A short distance from Steinbach there still exists Luther's Spring, so called from the

---

* The accounts differ. Some have it that this was Luther's own brother Jacob, and others that the Augustinian brother was still one of the company.

fact that he requested permission of his captors to dismount and drink of the clear-mountain-stream. Near the spring there formerly stood an ancient stately beech called the Luther Beech by the people in the vicinity. On March 18, 1841, it was overthrown by a violent storm, and only a stump of the old trunk remained, from which a living branch is still growing. The wood of the demolished tree was presented by the count Von Meiningen to the church at Steinbach, and a profitable trade is carried on from it. Larger and smaller fragments of it, with the authorized church-stamp attesting its authenticity, are sold to carvers and turners, who make various articles of it for collectors of relics. There is a billet of this tree also preserved in the Luther Room in Wartburg Castle. Near the remains of the tree which still stand the count Von Meiningen, in the year 1858, erected a square sandstone monument in the form of a Gothic tower with the inscription in front: "Here Dr. Martin Luther, on May 4, 1521, by order of Frederick the Wise, elector of Saxony, was seized and conveyed to the castle of Wartburg. 'He shall drink of the brook in the way: therefore shall he lift up the head' (Ps. cx. 7)." On the rear side: "Erected by Bernhard Erich Freund, count of Sachsen Meiningen, in the year 1858." On the right side: "'He that walketh righteously and speaketh uprightly, he shall dwell on high: his place of defence shall be the munitions of rocks' (Isa. xxxiii. 15, 16)." And on the left: "'The Lord is my rock, and my fortress, and my deliverer, my God, my strength, in whom I will trust' (Ps. xviii. 2)." A very significant monument indeed! As the place where he was seized cannot be distinctly determined at the present day, yet it seemed natural and correspondent with the design to erect the monument at the Luther Spring, the name of which, as is thought, undoubtedly must sustain a casual connection with the abduction of the Reformer. Much has been written to demonstrate the authenticity of this place, but it would require too much space to present the argument, nor would it be of any special interest to the general reader.

But we will leave the Luther Spring and follow the captive a few miles farther. Although aware that he would be rescued by his friends, yet he did not know whither they would conduct him. Weary from the long and rapid riding on horseback, the hospitable gate of the Wartburg was thrown wide open to the cavalcade at eleven o'clock at night.

Comfortable quarters were immediately assigned to the captive, and all necessary attention was paid to him. Several pages were constantly within call, and he fared more sumptuously than ever before. Frequently did he implore his generous guardian, the castellan Von Berlepsch, not to give himself so much solicitude about his comfort; but that officer had received orders which he was bound to obey, and, besides, he felt himself honored in having such a distinguished prisoner under his care. Everything was done to prevent a betrayal of his presence, and hence he assumed the name of "Squire George" and adapted his external appearance to the character and social position of the name he had taken.

"I have laid aside my monk's habit and have donned the vesture of a knight. I have allowed my hair and beard to grow, so that you would hardly recognize me; indeed, I am so changed that I scarcely know myself." Thus he writes to Spalatin, and in a letter to Melanchthon, on May 26, he writes: "I have nothing more to say, for I am a hermit, anchorite and real monk, yet not according to tonsure or vestment. You would take me for a knight and hardly know me." Besides allowing his beard, moustache and hair to grow long, he wore a red cap, a military cloak, and occasionally the sword of a knight, as well as huge boots and spurs.*

During the early period of his concealment

---

* Luther was painted by Lucas Kranach in this unusual garb. A poet of that day thus writes below a wood-cut of the picture:

"Zu Wartburg Doctor Luther war
Verborgen fast ein ganzes Jahr,
Ein grosser Bart ihm war gewachsen,
Wie damals trugen auch die Sachsen,
Und ganz verändert Sein Gestalt
War neun und dreysig Jahr gleich alt,
Gen Wittenberg geritten kam
Zu Nicolas Amsdorff, da er nahm
Die Herberg, eh er Seinen Bart
Hat abgelegt, als bald er ward
Von Lucas Kranach abgemalt
Also wie er ist hie gestalt."

no one saw him except a few persons connected with the castle, and even later he had very little intercourse with other people. Even his correspondence with friends was guarded with vigilant anxiety. In a letter to Amsdorf of May 12 he says: "I have recently written to my friends in Wittenberg, but I have followed better advice and torn up my letters, for it is not yet safe to write;" and in a later one, to Spalatin, he says: "I found some difficulty in having this despatched, for they are very apprehensive that it might become known where I am. Hence, if you think it will be for the honor of Christ, let it continue doubtful, or make it so, whether friend or foe has me in custody, and keep silent yourself; for, besides you and Amsdorf, it is not necessary for anybody to know whether I am living or dead." On July 15 he complains that he "had heard from Amsdorf that a secretary of Duke John had written to a lady in Torgau that he was at Wartburg Castle. Hence the report was spread all around, and the people would be convinced, because it came from the court. Whether the writer really knew it or presumed it, it would now be in vain to keep the secret. Thus Satan entraps us and betrays our cause."

In all his letters he omits the mention of the place of his sojourn. He dates "From my Desert," "From my Hermitage," "On the Hill," "In the Airy River," "In the Region of the Birds, which cheerfully sing in the trees and praise God day and night with all their strength."* But the majority of his letters are dated "From my Hermitage," "From my Patmos." The latter name he afterward used more frequently than any other. On one occasion he employed a little trickery to deceive his enemies as to the place of his concealment. In a letter to Spalatin he encloses another which was dated somewhere else, and which Spalatin was purposely to lose, so that it

---

* The dates "In the Region of the Birds" and "Among the Birds" are found only in some letters written in May. He who has stood on the Wartburg on some clear morning or calm evening of May and listened to the sweet warbling of the finches and nightingales, which to this day "praise God day and night" in that delightful region, will recognize in those dates something more than the bare design of keeping the secret of his residence, and will sympathize with the tender and refined emotions which swelled the heart of Luther.

might fall into the hands of his enemies. He was desirous that it should it come under the eye of Duke George in Dresden, who would eagerly betray and report the pretended secret.

Luther's sudden disappearance naturally created extraordinary anxiety and alarm. Many of his adherents feared that by the artful stratagem of his opponents he had been violently put out of the way; others hoped and wished that he had been somewhere concealed by his friends. Thus, in Eisenach, where numerous stories were in circulation, it was reported and believed that he had been seized and conveyed out of Franconia, not even dreaming that at the same time he was comfortably quartered within a few miles of their own city. One report was, that one of the counts Von Henneberg had captured him, but the count publicly made an indignant denial. None but Amsdorf and Spalatin knew where he was concealed. The former·learned it from Luther himself, who received permission from his custodian after a few weeks to write to him. The first letters which Luther wrote to some friends in Wittenberg were torn to pieces at the command of Von Berlepsch, who deemed it yet too early to hold any intercourse with the outer world. Melanchthon also must have known at least that Luther had not been murdered, for he communicated the glad intelligence to their common friend Wenzel Link, in Nurnberg: "Our dearest father is still alive."

On the other hand, his enemies and persecutors soon became painfully anxious lest the excitement of the people should grow greater and trouble ensue; hence they wished him back again. Luther heard of this apprehension of his enemies, and hence he writes to Spalatin in May or June: "The priests and monks, who, whilst I was yet free, raved about me and became almost insane in their persecution, are now so alarmed about my abduction that they begin to palliate their folly and want it to be forgotten. They cannot endure the popular feeling in my favor, and know not how to get out of the difficulty. . . . Is not the language of Moses true?—'The Lord shall fight for you, and ye shall hold your peace' (Ex. xiv. 14). A papist has written to the archbishop of Mayence, 'We have lost Luther, just as we desired, but the people are everywhere so excited that we are not sure of our lives if we do not hunt for him everywhere with lamps and bring him back again.'" He was joking, it is true, but how would it be if real earnest would follow his joke? Pretending prophets and soothsayers were summoned to divine the place of concealment, but Providence guarded Luther against all intrusion, and drew for a while a veil around this servant of God which no human eye could penetrate.

Luther, with his vivacious and manly spirit, accustomed to a bustling, stirring, vigorous activity, and overflowing with heartfelt sympathy in the fate of his friends in Wittenberg, felt himself very much cramped and out of place in his solitude and isolation. He had too many general interests confided to him to feel comfortable, shut out of all fellowship with the world. The feeling of relief from the threatening danger and his deliverance from the machinations of his enemies never entered his mind. He was willing at any moment to die a martyr to the cause, but the sudden seclusion from society, and the inability to take any public part in the affairs of the Church to which he saw himself condemned, were extremely distasteful to him, and this occasioned the deepest dejection. He writes to Spalatin: "I am unspeakably cast down, and my conscience torments me that, yielding to your advice and that of other friends, I suppressed my spirit in Worms and did not act the part of Elisha to those idols. They shall hear something quite different, if I should ever encounter them again." He often regretted the humility and reverential respect which restrained him from declaring his confession before the tyrants in a more fearless manner.

He soon began to long for greater freedom of spirit; he felt a painfully ardent desire for a higher and fresher activity in all that concerns the interests of humanity; and this involuntary confinement often filled him with sadness. "I am a wonderful prisoner, who sits here partly with my will and partly against my will—with my consent, because it is the Lord's will; against my consent, because I wish publicly to stand up for the word, but am not yet worthy of it." Thus he expressed himself on May 12 to John Agricola, and some days later to Melanchthon, to whom he sent a report of his literary labor: "I do not want you to be anxious about me. As far as my person is concerned, I am quite well; only that my mind is still disturbed and that the former weakness of spirit and of faith continues. My seclusion is of no account whatever; but for the honor of the divine word and for the strengthening of others as well as of myself, I would rather burn on glowing coals than rot, half living and yet not dead, in solitude."

At another time he writes: "Do you not pray that my flight, to which I unwillingly yielded, may turn out to the greater glory of God? I am very anxious to hear what you think of it. I fear that it may appear as though I retreated from the battle-field; but there was no evasion, and I could not resist the advice of friends. I would wish nothing better than this moment to expose myself to the most furious rage of my enemies."

As has been observed, Luther was well provided for on the Wartburg, and he was most kindly treated, as he often says in his letters. His relations to the castellan Von Berlepsch, notwithstanding their different social positions, were of the most pleasant character. The majority of the officials at that time were knights of high rank, but the generous heart of the chief bowed irresistibly to the brilliant genius of his distinguished captive, "whose eagle eye," as Erasmus designated it, encountered his own proud look, and whose enchanting discourse, conveyed in deep sonorous tones, won his custodian's admiration, and whose discriminating judgment and sparkling wit seasoned their mutual intercourse.

Besides the two pages of noble birth who waited upon Luther, the *personnel* of the castle consisted of two equerries, a secretary, the chaplain, a steward, a cook, a gatekeeper, two watchmen, a muleteer and a schoolmaster, who also officiated as vicar at an altar in the chapel.

But it occasioned silent uneasiness and saddened his delicate sensibility that he was entirely unaware at whose expense he was so generously supported in his exile. "Be not concerned that I may not be able to endure my banishment," he writes to Spalatin, August 15, "for it is nothing to me where I live, if I only do not become a burden to these people here. But I believe that I am living

LUTHER AT WARTBURG CASTLE. 47

here at the expense of our prince; otherwise I would not remain here an hour if I knew that I am consuming the provision of this man" (meaning the castellan), "although he cheerfully furnishes me everything I want. You would do me a favor by giving me certain information on this point; for I can conclude nothing from the noble sentiment of this man except that he supports me at the expense of the elector. But I am so inclined that I fear being burdensome where it is not really the case, and this anxiety is not inconsistent with a proper dignity."

Luther's despondency and the oppressive feeling of solitude were much aggravated by bodily indisposition. He was attacked by sickness soon after his arrival at the Wartburg. The want of exercise had disturbed his digestion and occasioned severe attacks of colic. This evil, from which he had already suffered at Worms, was not abated, but rather increased from day to day, and annoyed him through the whole summer. It was only toward autumn that he was relieved and restored to health.

He often complained to his friends of his

sufferings and severe pains. Let us his hear his own words: "I have not slept the whole night, and have no rest yet. If this evil continues as it has begun, it will become intolerable." He thus writes to Melanchthon in his first letter, May 12, and on June 10 to Spalatin: "My trouble from which I suffered in Worms has not yet left me, but has become worse. I suffer so severely that I doubt of help or cure. Thus the Lord chastens me, so that I am not without the cross. His name be praised! Amen." Again, on July 13, to Melanchthon: "It is now eight days that I neither write nor pray nor study, because I am terribly visited with temptations of the flesh and other grievous evils. If things do not improve, I shall publicly go to Erfurt, where you will see me or I see you, for I wish to consult a physician and a surgeon. I cannot endure it any longer; I would rather suffer ten great wounds than this calamity. Perhaps God is laying this severe infliction upon me, that He may tear me out of this wilderness to mingle with the people again." A few days later he expresses the same determination to seek medical aid in Erfurt to

LUTHER AT WARTBURG CASTLE.   49

Spalatin, who had sent him some remedies: "I have received everything safely, and have used the pills according to order. I feel somewhat relieved, but still have pains. I am apprehending the worst again. If the evil does not abate, I will go to Erfurt and employ a physician." In the mean time, the plague broke out in Erfurt, and the severity of his sickness had somewhat abated. "It was the occurrence of the plague," he writes to the same on July 31, "that prevents me from going to Erfurt. I feel somewhat better after taking much and strong medicine, but the condition of my digestive organs has not improved, and I judge that the affliction will grow worse, as the Lord is chastening me." It was only in the fall, as has been observed, that he could rejoice in the full restoration of his health. "My salutation and thanks for what you have sent. My sick body has reconciled itself to me, so that I have no more need of medicine. I am perfectly well as formerly. God be praised!" Thus he writes to Spalatin on October 7.

To this diary of his bodily condition must yet be added a brief history of a hunting-expedition of which he wrote to Spalatin on August 15: "Last week I was two days on the chase, and had a taste, for once, of the bitter-sweet enjoyments of these great gentlemen. We caught two hares and one pair of poor pheasants. Really a dignified employment for idle people! Here, among nets and dogs, I had my theological thoughts, and as much sport as the sight of such things made me, so also did the concealed mystery and picture fill me with sympathy and pain. For what does this picture represent but the devil through his ungodly masters and dogs —namely, the bishops and theologians—chasing and capturing innocent little animals? This picture of simple and believing souls was vividly represented to my sympathizing heart. Added to this was an effort to preserve the life of a little hare. I concealed it in my sleeve and withdrew myself a little distance from the company. In the mean time, the dogs had scented it, and bit it in the right leg through my coat, and finally killed it. Thus the pope and Satan rage and destroy redeemed souls, without any regard to my care. I am sick and tired of this sort of chase, and look upon that as much more pleasant in which bears, wolves, wild hogs, foxes, and the like—which represent ungodly teachers—are killed by spears and arrows. This I intend as my spiritual pleasantry with you, so that you consumers of game at court may know that ye also will be game in Paradise, which Christ, the best hunter, can scarcely capture and keep even with much trouble."

We can safely assume that Luther was permitted to wander occasionally outside of the castle for the restoration of his health and the enjoyment of fresh mountain-air: the history of the chase just related is evidence of the fact. It is likely, also, that in the course of time further excursions in the vicinity were allowed him, accompanied by a faithful and intelligent guide. The secret journey to Wittenberg at the end of the year would confirm this presumption, and even be a proof of it.

Luther is silent on this subject in all his letters from the Wartburg to his friends. It is only Mathesius who relates it, and, as it would appear, from Luther's own communication: "As our Luther diligently continues his studies and writing in his solitude and becomes exhausted, some of his friends advise him to take walks for exercise to improve his health and breathe fresh air. Hence they take him on the chase; sometimes he goes to gather strawberries; and, besides, they occasionally send with him an honest servant, a presumed knight or equerry, whose fidelity and knightly remonstrance he afterward highly lauds, because he warned him against taking off his sword in places of entertainment and immediately inspecting the books, so that the people may not look upon him as a scholar. Thus Dr. Luther went to several monasteries quite unknown. At Martsul he went among his friends, but they did not know Squire George; for that was what the equerry called him. He was recognized by some at Reinhardsborn. When the attendant observed that, he reminded his squire that he must not neglect the appointed business of the evening, and hastily left the place."

In the days of his deep despondency, to which his bodily sufferings and isolation naturally contributed much, Luther thought that the Evil One was persecuting him in every possible way, and would leave him no rest because he so faithfully and conscientiously labored in the cause of God. He complains of such temptations and conflicts of spirit even after he had been restored to health. On November 1, he thus writes to Spalatin: "There are many wicked and crafty devils about who will yet kill me. Pray that Christ may not abandon me;" and in the same style he expresses himself on the same day to his friend Gerbell, a lawyer in Strasburg: "Believe me that in this idle solitude I am assailed by thousands of devils. It is more difficult to fight these wicked spirits than the incarnate devils—that is, wicked men."

It is said that in 1546 he related the following story to some friends in Eisleben: "When, in 1521, I departed from Worms, and was seized near Eisenach and conveyed to the Wartburg, and was located in my Patmos, I had a room remote from all others, and nobody was allowed to come to me except two noble youths who twice a day brought me food. They had bought for me a sack of hazelnuts, of which I occasionally ate, and had them locked up in a chest. When I went to bed at night I undressed in the room, put out the light, went into my sleeping-chamber, adjoining, and laid down. Then the nuts began to play all manner of pranks. One after the other rose and struck hard against the rafters and rattled round my bed, but I was not disturbed about it. After I had nearly fallen asleep, such a rumbling was heard on the stairs, as if a great number of barrels were rolling down; and though I knew that the stairs were barred by chains of iron, so that no one could come up, still the casks were rolling down. I rose to see what was the matter, and the stairs were closed. Then I said, 'If it be thou, so be it;' and, commending myself to the Lord Jesus, of whom it is written (Ps. viii. 7), 'Thou hast put all things under his feet,' I again went to bed. At this time the wife of Hans von Berlepsch came to Eisenach, and, having heard that I was at the castle, was very desirous of seeing me; but that could not be. To accommodate her at the castle I gave up my chamber to her, and they provided another for me. During the night there was such a rattling in the room that she thought there were a thousand devils in it. But the best way to drive him away is to call upon Christ and to despise the devil: that he cannot bear. We must say to him, 'If thou art Lord over Christ, let it be so!' Thus I said to him at Eisenach."

Myconius, in his history of the Reformation, writes: " In the year 1538, Dr. Martinus related to us the whole account" (of his sojourn on the Wartburg) "in the house of John Löben at Gotha; so that Jonas, Pomeranus and all who were present were astounded. Many wonderful and interesting events occurred during his captivity, and among them was how the devil appeared twice to Luther at Wartburg in the form of a great dog that would tear him to pieces, but was overcome by the power of Christ."

Legends of various temptations of the devil, who repeatedly annoyed him during his translation of the Bible, are universally known and deeply impressed on the popular mind. They culminate in the one which reports Luther's hurling his inkstand at the devil, and which effectually drove him away. This legend is very vividly brought to the recollection of every visitor to Luther's room, where the celebrated and frequently-freshened ink-spot, now deeply sunk in the wall, is still exhibited, and keeps alive among the populace the famous old traditionary story. The oft-repeated but improbable story is that one day especially he fancied that he beheld Satan, filled with horror at his work, tormenting him and prowling about him like a lion ready to seize his prey. Luther, alarmed and incensed, snatched up his inkstand and flung it at the head of his enemy. The figure disappeared with a dismal howl, and the missile dashed in pieces against the wall.

It is worthy of remark that no contemporary historian of Luther mentions this affair, and it may be that some romantic reader may not thank the honest historian for breaking up the old popular illusion.*

All the biographies of Luther contain accounts of these legends, and Michelet devotes more than thirty pages to this subject. The

---

* On once observing to the show-woman at the Wartburg that Luther's ink must have been particularly good, to have retained its deep black color for over three hundred years, she with charming simplicity replied, *"Oh, sir, we freshen it up every now and then" !*

following remarks from D'Aubigné are judicious:

"Solitary and in ill-health, and saddened by the exertions of his enemies and the extravagances of some of his followers, seeing his life wear away in the gloom of that old castle,—he had occasionally to endure terrible struggles. In those times men inclined to carry into the visible world the conflicts that the soul sustains with its spiritual enemies.

"Luther's lively imagination easily embodied the emotions of his heart, and the superstitions of the Middle Ages had still, and continued to have through his life, some hold upon his mind.

"Satan was not, in Luther's view, an invisible, but real, being. He thought that he appeared to men as he appeared to Christ. Although the authenticity of many of the stories on this subject contained in *The Table-Talk* and elsewhere is more than doubtful, history must still record this failing in the Reformer.

"Never was he more assailed by these gloomy, ghastly ideas than in the solitude of the Wartburg. In the days of his strength he had braved the devil in Worms, but now his powers were somewhat broken. He was thrown aside; Satan was victorious in his turn; and, in the anguish of his soul, Luther imagined he saw his giant form towering before him, lifting his finger in threatening attitude, exulting with a bitter and hellish sneer and gnashing his teeth in fearful rage."

The papal anathema and the imperial edict, which denounced him as a recognized heretic, gave him but little uneasiness in his asylum. He several times alludes to the "terrible edict" in his first letters to Melanchthon, Amsdorf and Spalatin, but he is convinced that it will injure the cause of his adversaries. He regarded the political conflicts in which the emperor was entangled after the Diet as divine judgments upon him for his conduct in this affair. "The unhappy young man will never be prosperous, and will have to atone for the ungodliness of others, because, in Worms, following the advice of his wicked counsellors, he scorned and rejected the truth which was distinctly set before him. His misfortune will also comprehend Germany, because it also consented to the counsels of the ungodly." Thus Luther expresses himself almost sympathizingly for the emperor to Spalatin on July 15.

But the best evidences and demonstrations of his unterrified spirit, and of his unshaken confidence in the progress and final conquest of his righteous cause in spite of the ban and the edict, are the number of his writings, besides other labors, which he began and partly finished on the Wartburg.

His own natural inclination to activity, as well as the exertions of his enemies to undermine and overthrow the work of the Reformation already begun, did not allow Luther to rest or to keep silence in his seclusion. The timidity and lack of courage of some of his friends, also, or the untimely and intemperate zeal of others, compelled him several times to seize the pen either to encourage or to console or to rebuke them. Just as the apostles in prison, so had he whilst in custody, to edify and comfort the Church of the Lord. The letters which he wrote, particularly to Melanchthon, Spalatin and Amsdorf, testify the lively interest which he felt in the affairs of the outer world, especially in Wittenberg.

It would require more space than can here be spared to cite the various occasions of this correspondence and historically to illustrate the facts which drew from him these warm expressions of anxiety and sympathy. Only the more important of the writings which he began or finished on the Wartburg shall be noticed. Through them his voice rolled down from his mountain-retreat and reverberated through valley and plain, everywhere awakening the most absorbing interest.

Here, while the Roman See raged furiously at the audacious innovator's escape, he himself looked down securely from the platform of his dungeon-keep, finding in this quiet retreat full leisure to resume his flute, to sing his German psalms, to translate his Bible, and to thunder forth against the pope and the devil.*

After his arrival at that fortress, he immediately took the Bible in hand and studied it diligently in the Hebrew and Greek original text. After a few weeks had elapsed, several writings were ready for the press. The first

---

* Michelet.

LUTHER AT WARTBURG CASTLE. 61

was the exposition of Ps. lxviii., of which several verses were sung at public worship on Ascension Day and Whitsunday. Both these festivals he celebrated on the Wartburg, and devoted his leisure-time during this festival season to the illustration of this psalm, but without having any books or other helps besides the Bible at hand. It was finished on May 26, and, with a long and instructive letter, it was sent to Melanchthon at Wittenberg. On June 10 there followed to Spalatin, at the same time with his brief treatise *On Confession*, a commentary on the Magnificat, or Mary's song of praise (Luke i.), which had been commenced for Duke John Frederick before Luther set out for Worms, but was now finished on the Wartburg. The treatise *On Confession* was dedicated to the knight Franz von Sickingen, who was Luther's enthusiastic admirer.

At the same time there was published, together with the above, a translation of the one hundred and nineteenth psalm, with brief notes, and, as a continuation of the larger commentary of the Psalms in Latin, begun some time before, the exposition of the twenty-second was already finished on June 10 and sent to the printing-office in Wittenberg.

To these biblical labors also belongs the exposition of the Gospel of the Ten Lepers, which Duke John, who had heard of Luther's sojourn from the castellan, was very desirous of having, because it was thought it contained passages contradictory to his treatise *On Confession*. Luther executed this commission and sent the manuscript to Spalatin on September 17, with the request to employ some correct copyist, for his own handwriting must be kept secret, and then to send it to the duke. He also wished Spalatin to return the original, for he had no second copy, and could not himself employ any one else to copy it in order not to be betrayed.

The book was printed in the same year at Wittenberg, with a vigorous preface which showed the resoluteness of his spirit as distinctly as it severely scourged the selfishness of the papists and their lame defence of auricular confession. "I, a poor brother" (thus begins the preface), "have again kindled a fresh fire. I have bitten a great hole in the pocket of the papists by having attacked their doctrine of confession. Where shall I now stand? and where will they find enough sulphur, pitch, fire and wood to burn to ashes the poisonous heretic? They must certainly smash in the church windows, for some holy fathers and spiritual gentlemen preach that they must have fresh air to proclaim the gospel—that is, to defame Luther and cry 'Murder!' against him. They exclaim nothing but 'Death! death! death to the heretic! for he aims at overturning everything and destroying the whole spiritual profession in all Christendom.' I hope, if I should be worthy of it, that they may succeed in putting me to death and fill up the measure of their fathers; but it is not yet time; my hour has not come; before that I must still further provoke the brood of vipers and properly deserve death at their hands, that they may have reason to offer me up as a great sacrifice." "Confession," says Luther, "is neither based on Scripture nor was it observed in the times of the apostles: it is entirely a human invention. They accuse us of neglecting and condemning it, because we do not wish to confess and do not want to speak or hear of it. To this we reply, We confess our faults: we are poor sinners." He then proceeds to argue the subject, and shows finally that the chief reason why the papal priests so strenuously maintain the practice, against all Scripture and apostolic usage, is the immense revenue which auricular confession brings to the Church.

Thus thought and wrote Luther against this unscriptural doctrine and practice of Rome. He unceasingly contended for the purification of the Church from all human inventions, abuses and follies, like a genuine, resolute gospel-knight without fear and without reproach. No threats could intimidate this gospel-hero.

A translation and exposition of Ps. xxxvii., together with a consolatory epistle, he dedicated to his beloved congregation at Wittenberg on November 1, designating it as "the poor little flock in Wittenberg," demonstrating thereby his tender solicitude in behalf of the place, and of the church there gathered. He concludes the letter in these words: "By God's grace, I am as bold and resolute as I have ever been. I suffered for a while from sickness, but it has done no harm. . . . Be of good courage and fear nobody. The grace of God be with you. Amen!"

Besides these translations and explanations of various sections of the Bible, which were to serve for the instruction, consolation and elevation of Christian people, and at the same as preliminary to his translation of the Scriptures, he was also engaged in a learned theological controversy with some of his opponents. More than one sharp treatise was sent out into the world from the Wartburg. To that *On Auricular Confession*, which has been mentioned, there followed a reply to a book by Latomus, a theologian of Lyons, who undertook to secure the condemnation of the Lutheran doctrine by the theological faculty of that city. Luther most unwillingly entered upon the refutation of Latomus, but he felt himself compelled to engage in it. It was hastily written within the 8th and 20th of June, but it grew into a very important scientific treatise.

"You can scarcely believe how reluctantly I allowed myself to be torn away from my quiet and peaceful studies to which I have devoted myself here in my Patmos, and to apply my precious time to the useless gabble of this square-headed sophist." Thus speaks Luther in a letter to Justus Jonas when he sent the refutation to him in June, and at the end of the same letter he adds: "There! take the writing. How glad I am that it does not remain any longer with me!"

A new attack by Emser, with whom Luther had for some time conducted a controversy upon the universal priesthood, was also refuted from the Wartburg in a treatise entitled *Contradiction of an Error committed by the most highly learned Mr. Hieronymus Emser*, etc., in which he finishes off his opponent in a still sharper and clearer style than before. The theological faculty of Paris, the highest scientific and scholastic authority of the Church of the Middle Ages, had issued a decree of condemnation against Luther's doctrine, and Melanchthon had undertaken the refutation of it. Of this Luther writes to him on July 13: "I have a notion of translating into German, with accompanying notes, your *Apology* against the asses at Paris, together with their nonsense." (By this he means their condemnation of his doctrine.) This was done.

The translation, with a sharp epilogue and biting notes, appeared in the same year, under the title *Counter-Condemnation against the Theologians of Paris*. In the epilogue, among other things, it is said: "Although my dear Philip has answered them in a masterly manner, he has treated them too mildly and scourged them too gently. It is plain that I must use a woodman's axe in splitting these coarse blocks, and slash them to pieces; otherwise they will not feel it."

Still more sharp and vehement was his attack upon Archbishop Albert of Mayence. He had re-established the traffic in indulgences in his capital; he had also punished some priests who had married, and had kept a priest a long time in prison on this account, until he consented to abandon his wife. In addition, it was reported that he sold the privilege of keeping concubines to the priests for money, and by his own conduct in regard to his vow of chastity, he gave offence and caused public scandal. Against this tyranny and abomination Luther wrote a treatise called *Against the Idol in Hallé*, which was finished on November 1.

But previous to this, the archiepiscopal counsellor Capito had been in Wittenberg and made his appearance at the electoral court. By certain representations and promises he prevailed upon certain persons to have his master spared, and not to be attacked by any public writing. Luther's protector, the elector, was also himself decidedly opposed to Luther engaging in controversy against one of the first princes of the empire, who could easily disturb and imperil the peace of the realm. Spalatin had informed Luther of this, and told him that the elector would not suffer anything to be written against the archbishop. To this Luther replied, November 11: "My salutation. A more unpleasant letter than your last I have scarcely ever read. I not only delayed my reply, but I also resolved not to send any answer. In the first place, I cannot endure it that, as you say, the prince will not allow that anything shall be written against the Mayencer, and that the public peace will be disturbed. I would rather overturn you and the prince himself, and all creation besides. If I have resisted the archbishop's creator, the pope, why should I spare his creature? You talk very prettily about avoiding a disturbance of the public peace, and yet are willing that the eternal peace of God should be disturbed by him through his ungodly and outrageously immoral conduct. Not so, my Spalatin; not so, my prince; but for the sake of Christ's flock the most vigorous opposition must be made to that eminently dangerous wolf. To this end I hereby send you a writing which was already finished when your letter came, which did not move me to alter a word in it; but you may submit it to Melanchthon for inspection. Hand it to him, but do not advise against its publication, for I will assuredly not listen to any such counsel."

But Spalatin, notwithstanding this explicit declaration, withheld the writing, and Luther subsequently gave ear to the representations of his friends and consented to the postponement of its publication for a season. But, instead of that, on December 1, he sent a private letter to the archbishop with the threat that if he did not immediately abolish the traffic in indulgences he would publish the affair to the whole world. He demands an explicit answer within fourteen days, or he would most certainly bring out his book *Against the Idol in Hallé*. He received the answer demanded; which is a very distinct evidence what a power for the elector, the archbishop and cardinal of Mayence, the secluded monk on the Wartburg had already become. This answer was accompanied by a letter from Capito, in which he shields his master and intimates that the archbishop himself would employ measures for the promotion of the gospel, but in a manner different from that which the Wittenberger pursued.

Luther was little edified by this epistle. His sincere and candid mind demanded uprightness and honesty, truth and conscientiousness; he could not, and would not, fully believe and trust either the archbishop or his counsellor. At the end of his letter to Capito he unreservedly says: "I did not wish to answer your cardinal, because I could not safely follow a middle course in not praising or censuring his dissimulation or his sincerity. But from you he will learn what Luther's spirit is; and if I should learn that he acts uprightly and honestly, I will abase myself before him and fall at his feet."

Amid these vexatious circumstances, it afforded him unspeakable pleasure to hear that the Augustinians in Wittenberg had adopted his views and doctrine in their church arrangements, and had abolished private and auricular confession. As an expression of his pleasure he dedicated to them, for their encouragement and growth in the faith through unity, a little book entitled *The Abuse of the Mass*. It is worthy of observation that at the close of it he alludes to an ancient German legend relating to the elector of Saxony, Frederick the Wise. Luther thus reports it: " When I was a child, I often heard a prophecy in this country that the emperor Frederick would redeem the holy sepulchre at Jerusalem; and it is the nature of prophecy to be fulfilled before it is understood, and it always has respect to something different from that which the language indicates to the people. Hence it appears to me that this prophecy is fulfilled in our princely duke Frederick of Saxony; for what else can be understood by the holy sepulchre than the Holy Scriptures, in which the truth of Christ, killed by the papists, was lying buried, which the mendicant orders and inquisitors of heretics so carefully guarded that no disciple of Christ could come and steal it? For concerning the grave in which our Lord lay, God cares about as much as he does about the cattle in Switzerland. Now, no one can deny that through Duke Frederick, the elector of Saxony, the living word of the gospel has come forth to you; . . . and although he is now not an emperor, yet it is enough for the fulfilment of the prophecy that at Frankfort he was unanimously chosen by the electors as emperor, and would have been emperor if he had desired it. It is of no account to God how long a man is emperor if he only has been elected."

November 21 is the date of a preface and dedication to his dear father, Hans Luther, of a little book entitled *M. Luther's Judgment concerning Monastic Vows*. It was written in Latin and translated into German by Justus Jonas, and was brought out, as Luther writes to Spalatin, for the purpose of rescuing young people from the hell and filth of celibacy. Its truthful thoroughness and impressive force created great sensation in and outside of the cloisters.

Toward the end of November, Luther unexpectedly made his appearance in Wittenberg. We do not know to a certainty what was the occasion of this suddenly-conceived and hastily-executed tour. Naturally, it received the sanction of the castellan, but it was done entirely without the knowledge and will of his sovereign the elector. But, not to displease his princely patron and protector, Luther earnestly requests that his departure from the Wartburg, as well as his return, should be kept secret. He remained in Amsdorf's house in Wittenberg for several days in seclusion, and saw no one but a few trusted friends. How happily these days of renewed association with his friends, after so long a separation, after such a painful solitude and numerous anxieties, must have passed in earnest conversation and fraternal intercourse!

Luther here learned for the first time that Spalatin held back some writings from the hands of those who had engaged to publish them, because he feared that they might do more harm than good. They were those *On Monastic Vows, On the Mass* and *Against the Tyrant of Mayence*. He wrote to Spalatin from Wittenberg, and rebuked him most severely: "I came to Wittenberg, and among my delightful enjoyments in the company of my friends I found but one drop of wormwood, and that was that nobody had seen or heard of the books and letters. . . . My desire is that what I have written shall be published, if not in Wittenberg, yet somewhere else. If the copies are lost, or if you have held them back, I shall be very much displeased, and shall hereafter write much more severely on these subjects. For he who may destroy dead paper cannot as easily quench the spirit of a man." However, we have already heard that Luther yielded to the prudent counsel of his friends, and finally consented to the judgment of those at the electoral court to do whatever they deemed best.

After his return to the Wartburg, he immediately wrote a pamphlet called *A Faithful Admonition to all Christians to guard against Sedition and Revolt.* This was probably occasioned by certain impressions and reports he had received and heard during this tour and in Wittenberg. It was sent to Spalatin early in December, with the wish that it might be printed and published as soon as possible. It is also likely that at this time he finished his translation and comments on the papal sacramental bull, or, as it is usually styled, Bulla Cœnæ Domini, from its first words in the Latin copy. This decree, which contains terrible curses against all opponents, was annually renewed and proclaimed amid certain imposing formalities on Green Thursday. Luther himself found a place in it on the preceding Green Thursday, and he was fiercely denounced. He published a translation of it, with notes, as a New Year's gift to the pope. He also added to it the tenth psalm, with notes, as a contrasted likeness of popery. The title of this remarkable treatise sufficiently characterizes its tone and contents: *Bulla Cœnæ Domini—that is, the Bull of the Evening Carousals of the most holy Lord the Pope*, *translated into German for a New Year's gift to the most holy Roman See. Ps. x. 7: His mouth is full of cursing and deceit and fraud: under his tongue is mischief and vanity.* The exposition of Psalm x. concludes with these words: "I trust that as everybody will see that this psalm pictures popery, that the pope does precisely as is therein described, and that no other government since the beginning of the world is like his, so will every one come to the conclusion that no other Antichrist may be expected. It is impossible that there should be a more corrupt system on earth, and that ruins more souls than that of the pope, saying nothing about his extortion of the worldly property of the people. Hence we must earnestly pray to God against this head-knave of all the enemies of God, until God come and deliver us from him. Let every Christian say, Amen!"

Amid these uninterrupted, diversified, and in part exciting, literary labors, there is one which Luther began soon after his going to Wartburg, and which was resumed after all his interruptions and annoyances and continued to the middle of November with intense energy and delight. It was the preparation of his *House Postils.* It consists of an exposition of the Epistles and Gospels for Sundays and holy days, and it was the first collection of Protestant sermons in the German language, and, next to the translation of the New Testament, is the most beautiful and ripest fruit of his silent leisure and seclusion from the world. Luther himself subsequently designates it as the best book he ever wrote. "Even the papists," says he, "like it."

But his crowning work on the Wartburg was unquestionably the translation of the New Testament. Of his determination to perform this work he speaks for the first time in a letter of December 18 to John Lange in Erfurt: "I will remain here in my seclusion until Easter. In the mean time, I will continue the *Postils*, and intend also to translate the New Testament into German, which our friends urge upon me. I hear that you also are at work upon it; continue as you have begun. Oh that every town had its interpreter, and that all tongues, hands, eyes, ears and hearts might be employed about this one book!"

To Amsdorf he writes, January 13, 1522: "I am going to translate the Bible, although therein I have undertaken a work which exceeds my strength. I know now what translating means, and why it has not until now been undertaken by any one who has set his name to it. But the Old Testament I cannot touch unless you are present and help me. Indeed, if I could have a secret chamber at your house, I would come at once, and with your help undertake the whole of it, from the beginning; and that would be a translation worthy of being read by all Christians, for I hope we would give to our Germany a better translation than the Latins have. It is a great work and worthy of the united exertions of us all, for it would promote the universal welfare of the whole Church."

We see that Luther laid hold of his work with earnestness and zeal, but what untiring energy and perseverance, what passionate devotedness and astounding industry, were necessary to complete the smaller, but not lighter, work of the translation of the New Testament, in the two months, January and February, until his leaving the Wartburg at the beginning of March! "I have translated not only the Gospel of John, but the whole New Testament, in my Patmos; but now Philip and I have begun to file it off, and, with God's help, it will be a nice work; and that I may make a beginning at once I want you to get for us from the people at court the names, forms and, if possible, a sight of the precious stones mentioned in Rev. xxi."

Then he reports to Spalatin on March 30, soon after his return from the Wartburg, and begs for his help and co-operation in the work, but that he must furnish only plain and simple expressions, for the language of the court and the castle could not be admitted into a book that was intended for the people and must be clothed in simple, popular words. As soon as he had revised the translation with the help of his dear friend, it was put to press, probably by Melchior Lotther, at Wittenberg, who seemed, however, to be proceeding too slowly for the impatient Luther, and he zealously hurried him on. It was finished on September 21, and this day was for many years celebrated by Bugenhagen and others as the festival of the Bible translation. The first edition was folio size and illustrated with numerous wood-cuts by Lucas Kranach.

In a few weeks the whole edition of three thousand copies was spread abroad in all countries. A nobleman who had returned from Jerusalem some time after showed Luther a copy which he had bought in that city. Numerous editions in various sizes were soon published.

From this brief bibliographical report of his literary labors at the Wartburg we have reason to be amazed at the zeal and industry which he displayed in the work of the Reformation even in his seclusion, and at the sympathy he felt and the co-operation he extended to everything that concerned the Church and the fate of his friends, adherents and fellow-laborers. "For my Germans," he wrote November 1 to his friend Gerbell, "I have been born; them will I serve." And this idea he faithfully carried out in his asylum in that fortress. The Bible translation which he there began, and in part finished, gives sufficient proof of it. It is the greatest creative act of the great Reformer. By it the Bible has been planted in the heart of the German people, and has become not only a reading-book, but a book that is read. With this book he laid the foundation-stone of the whole reformation-work, and at the same time renewed and established the language of Germany.

The events which were gradually in preparation in Wittenberg during Luther's absence, and which culminated into full activity in the year 1522, and which recalled Luther to public life, we will not here consider in detail. They lie outside of the Wartburg and properly belong to the history of the Reformation. Carlstadt had put himself at the head of the movement in Wittenberg. His too rash zeal in abolishing church abuses, and the violence and inconsiderateness by which he sought to prosecute his designs, had occasioned great disturbances, which met with the most decided disapprobation of the most faithful adherents of the Lutheran doctrine and threatened to lead to the most disastrous results. The general apprehension and excitement in Wittenberg were much increased when Carlstadt, in order to prosecute his reforms in the church life, combined with some other religious fanatics—the so-called prophets of Zwickau and the Augustinian preacher Gabriel Didymus. These fanatics claimed the gift of divine inspiration. They abolished infant baptism and the doctrine of the Trinity and rejected all human learning. Carlstadt, at the head of a crowd of students and citizens, stormed the castle church and demolished the pictures and altars, and everything else that was connected with Romish worship.

Luther heard of these rash proceedings, and his mighty heart was fired with holy zeal. On March 19, 1522, he thus wrote to Wenceslaus Link: "Satan has broken into my sheepfold, and has taught that the freedom of the spirit may be used as an occasion to the flesh —that, disregarding the requirements of love, any and every thing presumably good may be done by a hard-hearted and wicked rabble. Carlstadt and Didymus have set up these abominations. These reasons have compelled me to return; so that, if Christ wills it, I may destroy the sport of the devil." Many friends of the cause also entreated him to come to Wittenberg to put a stop to these shameless proceedings.

Luther apprehended the peril to which these fanatical spirits were exposing his reformation-work. We can easily imagine his painful anxiety in that narrow chamber on the Wartburg. From there he saw the fiery heavens, and the flames reflected from the burning of his church at Wittenberg, to which he was attached with all his soul, and which he wished gradually to restore to its primitive purity; there he heard the tolling of the bells which summoned help and the despairing cry of friends. What was he to do? He resolved to go to Wittenberg to extinguish the flames of revolt with his own voice and earnest entreaty. Already, at the end of February, he intimated this determination to his sovereign and protector: "God willing, I want to be there myself. I hope your Electoral Highness will not oppose me."

The elector sent an officer of his court—Johann Oswald—to dissuade him from returning to Wittenberg. He informed Luther that he might have the privilege of giving his advice to the Wittenbergers on the subject of the disturbances, but that on no account should he appear there in person, because the pope and the emperor might demand the delivery of him into their hands; in which case the elector would not know how to get out of the dilemma. But his resolution could not be shaken. His conscience would not allow him to be dissuaded from his settled purpose, although a heroic faith was necessary to sustain him; for the imperial edict had not yet been recalled, and any villain had the right to murder him wherever found. That he was not intimidated by any fear of peril, and that he regarded his departure as a divine command which was of more serious concern to him than that of his sovereign, though faithfully devoted to him, appears from his own words. "Yes," says he, "I am bound to suffer death for them" (the souls of men); "that I will also freely and cheerfully do by God's grace. God compels and calls and gives me reasons for it. It must and will be so. So let it be in the name of Jesus Christ, the Lord of life and death." In this, as in all other things, he did not seek his own glory or that of the world, but God's glory alone.

On March 3, Squire George left the Wartburg alone, dressed in knightly vestments and with full beard and sword. In Borna, near Leipzig, on March 5, he informed the elector in a letter of his proceeding, which in strongest terms expressed his unshaken courage, his indomitable will, unawed by threats, his confidence in God and his assurance of faith.

It was indeed a courageous step which he then ventured, on his own account, without permission—indeed, against the order of his exalted master and patron—to re-enter upon public life and to return to Wittenberg, there to protect the work of his Reformation from peril. Well may the deepest anxieties have agitated his soul during this retirement, but we have sufficient evidence how he maintained his cheerful fearlessness and tranquillity from his accidentally meeting two Swiss students in the tavern of the Black Bear in Jena. John Kessler of St. Gall, who afterward became a Reformer in his own country, had left Switzerland in company with a friend, John Reutiner, to travel to the University of Wittenberg. According to the custom of poor students, they travelled on foot, and one afternoon arrived at Jena wearied and thoroughly soaked with rain and splattered with mud. Denied access to all the taverns, they were about leaving the town to proceed to a neighboring village to spend the night. They were met by a man who kindly inquired where they were going at so late an hour; and when they related to him their sad case, he directed them to a tavern outside of the town, called "The Black Bear." There they were taken in. In the guest-room there sat a man alone in a corner, with an open book lying before him, in which he was reading. Immediately he saluted them very politely, and requested them to take a seat at the same table; before that, they had seated themselves on a bench at a distance, on account of their soiled clothes. The man invited them to partake of some refreshments with him, which they did not refuse. They presumed he was an equerry, for he wore a little cap of red leather, breeches and doublet; he had a sword by his side; his right hand rested on the pommel, his left grasped the hilt. He inquired where they were from; but, without waiting for an answer, he said, "You are Swiss, but what is the place of your residence in Switzerland?"

They replied, "St. Gall."

He continued:

"As you are going to Wittenberg, as I learn, you will find some good countrymen of yours there; for instance, Jerome Schurf and his brother Dr. Augustin."

"We have letters to them," said the students, and asked whether Luther had returned to Wittenberg.

"I have certain information," was his reply, "that Luther at the present time is not in Wittenberg, but that he is soon to be there. But Philip Melanchthon is there, and teaches the Greek language." Then he exhorted the young men to devote themselves diligently to the study of the Greek and Hebrew languages, for which Wittenberg afforded peculiar facilities.

They expressed their determination to give themselves no rest until they had seen and heard the man who had attacked the priesthood and the mass, and they added that their parents had assigned them to the clerical profession and they were anxious to know all about the condition of things.

"Where have you studied?" asked the equerry.

"At Basel."

"Well, what is the state of affairs in Basel? I feel much interested in that school. Is

Erasmus there yet? What is he doing?" he asked.

"As far as we know, things go on well in Basel. Erasmus is still there; but nobody knows what he is doing, for he keeps himself very˙ secluded from society."

"But what do they think of Luther in Switzerland?" inquired the stranger.

"As everywhere else, people have different opinions concerning him. Some cannot exalt him high enough, and thank God that he has revealed his truth through him and exposed their errors; others condemn him as an intolerable heretic, particularly the clergy."

"I understand it well," he replied. "It is the priests."

During this conversation the stranger excited the curiosity of the students. His intelligent observations, particularly his acquaintance with the Schurfs, Melanchthon and Erasmus, appeared remarkable to them; and their astonishment became still greater when one of them took in his hand the little book lying on the table and looked at it. It was a Hebrew Psalter. He laid it down again, when the equerry took it to himself.

"I would part with one of my fingers," resumed the student, "if I understood that language."

"You might easily learn it," said the stranger, "if you diligently studied it. I also desire to improve in it, and read it daily."

It had now become quite dark. Then the landlord came into the room and approached the table where the students were seated. When he observed their anxiety about Luther, he said, "Dear friends, you would have been favored with a sight of him if you had been here two days ago, for he was seated at this very table."

"That chagrined us very much, and we were angry with ourselves for having delayed so long, and blamed the bad roads, which hindered our progress. Yet it gratifies us very much that we are in the same house and seated at the same table where he was.

"The landlord laughed and went away. After a short time he called me out of doors," continues Kessler in his narrative, "and I was alarmed, thinking that he was going to call me to account for something improper I had said or done. Then he said to me, 'Since I certainly know that you are so anxious to see and hear Luther, I tell you he is the man who is at the table with you.' I thought he was playing a joke upon me, and told him that he wanted to gratify my desire to see Luther with a delusion. But he assured me again that he spoke the truth; but he requested me to act as though I did not know it.

"I returned to the room, but could not restrain myself from whispering to my companion, 'The landlord tells me that is Luther.' But he was incredulous, and replied, 'Perhaps he said it was Hutten and you did not understand him distinctly.' As his dress reminded me more of Hutten than of Luther, who was a monk, I let myself be persuaded that the landlord had said 'Hutten,' for the beginning of the names sounds somewhat similar.

"In the mean time, two merchants entered the tavern and took off their cloaks and spurs. One of them then laid an unbound book upon the table. The equerry asked what sort of book that was.

"'It is Dr. Luther's exposition of the Gospels and Epistles, just printed and published. Have you not seen it?'

"'I shall soon also get it,' was his only reply.

"Then came the landlord and announced that supper was ready. We, however, requested him to prepare something for us apart.

"'Dear sir, only take your seats at the table: I'll see that all is right.'

"When the stranger heard that, he said, 'Come, I will pay the landlord.'

"During the supper he spoke so edifyingly and so kindly that the merchants and we were more interested in him than in the meal. He also spoke of the approaching Diet at Nurnberg, and thought that nothing good would result from it, as the great lords were more concerned about balls and frolics in general than about the word of God. 'But I hope,' he continued, 'that the pure truth and word of God will produce more fruit among our children and posterity than among their parents, in whom error has taken deep root which cannot be easily eradicated.'

"The merchants also expressed their opinions, and the older of the two said, 'I am nothing but a simple, unlearned layman, and do not altogether understand these things; but, as it strikes me, Luther must be either an angel from heaven or a devil from hell. I would cheerfully spend ten guilders if I could only confess to him, for he could properly instruct my conscience.'

"Then the landlord approached us and said secretly, 'Be not concerned about the cost. Martinus has paid for your supper.' That pleased us vastly—not because of the money or the meal, but because *this* man had entertained us at his expense.

"After supper the merchants rose and went to the stable to see that their horses were well groomed. In the mean time, the stranger was with us in the room alone. We thanked him for his kindness, and said that we had taken him to be Ulrich von Hutten.

"'I am not he,' he replied; and to the landlord, who had just entered, he remarked, 'I have become a nobleman this evening, for these Swiss take me to be Ulrich von Hutten.'

"The landlord replied, 'You are not he, but you are Martin Luther.'

"He laughed and observed, 'These take

me for Hutten, and you for Luther; I should properly be called Martinus Marcolfus.'

"Then he rose, threw his cloak over his shoulders, took leave, and, shaking us by the hands, said, 'When you get to Wittenberg, salute for me Dr. Hieronymus Schurf.'

"'Cheerfully and willingly will we do it,' said we; 'but how shall we call you, so that he may understand the salutation?'

"'Say nothing more than "*He who is to come salutes you.*" He will comprehend the words.' With these words he left and retired to rest.

"After that the merchants again returned to the room, and wondered who the guest was that was at table with them. The landlord insisted that it was Luther, and at last they were persuaded of it, but were sorry that they had spoken so unbecomingly in his presence. They said that in the morning they would rise early and apologize to him, as they did not know him; and that occurred.

"In the morning they found him in the stable; and Martinus, in reply to their remarks, said, 'You said that you would cheerfully spend ten guilders for Luther if you could confess to him. If you did so, you would soon find out whether I am Martin Luther.' And, to avoid being further recognized, he mounted his horse and rode off toward Wittenberg.

"After our arrival at Wittenberg we went immediately to Dr. Schurf to deliver our letters to him. On entering the room we found Martin just as we had seen him at Jena, together with Philip Melanchthon, Justus Jonas, Nicolas Amsdorf, Dr. Augustin Schurf, who related to him what had occurred in that place during his absence.

"He saluted us and smiled, and, pointing with his finger, said, 'This is Philip Melanchthon, of whom I spoke to you.'

"Philip then turned to us and asked many questions, which we answered as well as we could. And thus we met those great men, to our high gratification."

This is the narrative of Kessler's and his friend's interview with Luther at the Black Bear.

During this journey he encountered a papal priest at Erfurt, who boasted that he could point out a hundred errors in Luther's doctrines, but when challenged to the task he retired in confusion.

Luther did not return to the Wartburg, but remained at Wittenberg and prosecuted with untiring industry to the end of his days, the stupendous work which Providence had entrusted to his hands.

The elector submitted to what he could not prevent, especially as Luther's arrival at Wittenberg occasioned the highest gratification, even jubilant exultation, and contributed also to the restoration of the public tranquillity. The elector sent to him the Jurist Jerome Schurf, who conveyed his gracious salutation; but he was instructed also to procure from Luther a written statement of the reasons why he returned to Wittenberg and an assurance that it was done without electoral consent, and, moreover, that he would not be an encumbrance to any one. The statement was to be so worded that it might be publicly shown, and Schurf was enjoined to keep the whole affair of his mission a secret. Luther was also to be informed that for several good reasons he would not be permitted to preach in the castle church.

Schurf reported the result of his interview with "the worthy Martin Luther," at that time the real apostle and evangelist of Christ, and presented to His Grace Luther's writing, in which he gave his reasons for returning. They chiefly were that he was urgently called by the church in Wittenberg; that during his absence the devil had attacked his flock, which attacks he could not repel by writing; and that he apprehended a general commotion among the German people, which he thought he could prevent by his personal presence. He humbly deprecated any want of respect for the emperor or the elector, but that he felt irresistibly impelled to pursue that course. Accompanying this letter was a note in which he begged the elector that if the letter should not be satisfactory, he would graciously please to furnish a draft himself, declaring, however, that he did not object to the publication of his own letter, for he had said nothing which he was afraid to let the whole world know, and for which he would not suffer any penalty. The elector was pleased with the letter in general, only he suggested a few verbal alterations and additions; one of which was that in speaking of the emperor he should announce him as "the Most Gracious."

Luther agreed to everything, and yet he could not suppress the following expressions in a letter to Spalatin: "I hereby send the letter to the elector. . . . One demand chagrins me, and that is that I must call the emperor 'my Most Gracious Lord;' for the whole world knows that he has been very *ungracious* to me, and everybody will laugh at this open duplicity. But I will prefer being laughed at and accused of deception rather than resist the expressed wish of the elector, though it be his infirmity. But I satisfied my conscience with the thought that it is the universal custom to give the emperor his ordinary title, even if he be very ungracious and provoking to some. Above all things I despise duplicity, and I have up to this time yielded enough. There will come a time when I shall speak more freely and candidly."

CONCLUSION.

In this little book we have for the most part taken only that into the account which

Luther himself has recited in his own letters. All more recent reports from other hands have been purposely omitted. The design was not to present a merely colored and unauthentic picture, but a true and trustworthy narrative drawn from reliable resources. Luther's life and works in this fortress do not need the help of legend and fiction, and the Wartburg still stands renowned for the asylum which it afforded to the Reformer of the Christian Church who was anathematized by the pope and outlawed by the emperor, but whose memory is dearly cherished and his name revered by an admiring world.

LUTHER AT COBURG.

FROM THE GERMAN

OF

PFEILSCHMIDT,

WITH ADDITIONS.

BY

J. G. MORRIS, D.D., LL.D.

PHILADELPHIA:
LUTHERAN PUBLICATION SOCIETY.
1882.

Copyright, 1882.

WESTCOTT & THOMSON,
Stereotypers and Electrotypers, Philada.

CONTENTS.

Æsop's Fables, 29, 63.
Agricola, John, 20, 50.
Altenburg, 20.
Antonia de Serva, 12.
Apology, 57, 58, 116.

BARCELONA, peace of, 9.
Birds, kingdom of, 27.
Bologna, 9, 12.
Brück, 12.
Bugenhagen, 14.

CAMBRAY, peace of, 8.
Campegi, legate, 60.
Caspar, Dr., 67.
Charles V., 8.
Clement VII., 9.
Coburg castle, 5, 16.
  decoration of, 7.
  amusements at, 29.
  loneliness at, 35.
Confutation, Catholic, 100, 103.
Conrad Cordatus, 17.

Corpus Christi festival, 55, 74.

DAWS, assembly of, 27.
Desert, 27.
De Wette, 27.
Diet of Augsburg, 10, 42.
Duke Ernest, 6.

ECK, 99.
Ehrenberg, 6.
Ein feste Burg, 29.
Elector John, 35.
  arrival at Augsburg, 40.
  letter to emperor, 51.
Emperor's delay, 22, 44, 68.
  entrance into Augsburg, 60.
  forbids preaching, 73, 75.
  moderation of, 82.

FAST days, 55.
Francis I., 8.

HANS VON DOLZIGK, 20.
Hausman, Nicolas, 17.

CONTENTS.

INNSPRUCK, emperor at, 34.
JOHN THE CONSTANT, 11, 13.
John Frederick, 12, 19.
Jonas, 14.
Journey to Torgau, 21.

KATHARINE, Luther's wife, 63.
King Ferdinand, 66.

LANDGRAVE PHILIP, 73, 108.
Luther at Coburg, 5, 7, 23, 24.
  reply to papists, 15.
  his influence, 24.
  writings at, 45, 46, 48, 104, 105.
  death of his father, 48, 69, 97.
  sympathy of, 67.
  visits to, 68, 70.
  impatience, 79.
  firmness, 95, 115.
  prayer, 96.
  on translation, 125.
  ring, 128.
  leaves Coburg, 139.
  letters from, *passim*.

MANTUA, 34.
Margrave George, 73.
Maria, queen of Hungary, 102.

Mass, 83.
Melanchthon, 14, 61, 62, 64, 123.
Mercurinus, 46.
Michael Kellner, 51.

NURNBERG council, 135.

PFIZER, Life of, 29.
Philip of Hesse, 12, 50, 55.
Preaching at Augsburg, 51.
Princes, firmness of, 86.

RETINUE to Coburg, 20.

SCHNEPF, chaplain, 51.
Spalatin, 20, 21.
Sultan Soliman, 9.
Swabach, 15.
Sybilla of Cleves, 21.

TETRAPOLITANA, 121.
Torgau Articles, 15.
Turks, 10.

URBANUS RHEGIUS, 50.

VEIT, DIETRICH, 29.
Vincentius Pimpinelli, 83.
Visits to Luther, 68.

WEIMAR, 21.
Wenceslaus Link, 63.
Wittenberg, 14.
Worms, edict of, 16.

ZWICKAU, 17.

LUTHER AT COBURG.

CHAPTER I.

FROM THE IMPERIAL PROCLAMATION FOR THE DIET OF AUGSBURG TO THE ARRIVAL OF LUTHER IN COBURG.

(January 1 to April 16, 1530).

COBURG CASTLE—at the present time designated as "The Fortress"—is one of the most interesting and beautiful remains of the Middle Ages which have escaped the desolations of war and the corroding tooth of time. It is situated on an eminence a short distance east of the city of Coburg, and from its towers it furnishes to the lover of nature a view of the most enchanting landscape for miles around. It is especially memorable from the fact that it was here that Luther lived for six months during the session of the Diet of Augsburg.

The oldest records date its erection as far back as A. D. 991, and for four hundred years it was the princely residence of many German rulers, some of whom improved it by various extensive and costly additions; but for many years it was suffered to fall into decay. In 1547, Duke Ernest built another castle, which he called "Ehrenberg," in the city, and the old fortress was used as a prison and a warehouse of cast-off furniture and other useless articles. The beautiful sculpture in wood and the splendid wainscoted ceilings were covered with whitewash and had in part fallen down; the magnificently-oramented doors were hanging loose on their hinges; the rich collection of armor—of great historical value—was corroded with rust and thrown carelessly in damp vaults; so that everything was on the fast road to destruction.

In 1837 the enlightened duke Ernest determined to restore the old castle to its former splendor, and employed the best artists of Germany to execute the work; and now the ancient halls are exhibited to the admiring beholder in their primitive grandeur. The duke was especially desirous that Luther's residence here should be worthily commemorated, and ordered the room which the Reformer principally occupied to be decorated in a style befitting the man and the place. The walls are adorned with life-size portraits of Luther and of his wife, painted on a ground of gold, with those of Melanchthon, Bugenhagen, Jonas, Brück and other distinguished men of the time. Many other ornamental figures, coats-of-arms, mottoes, inscriptions, and other devices, on dark gold ground, decorate the walls and ceiling.

The residence of Luther in this place from April 16 to the 5th or 6th of October, 1520, is an event of no less interest and importance than any in the history of the Reformation. The diversified experience of his inner life, and his activities *as a Christian, Reformer, translator* and *expounder* of the Scriptures, *German patriot, husband* and *father, friend, author, humorist* and *poet*, were developed in no period of his eventful life to a fuller extent than in the brief space of these six months; and yet, on the other hand, what a unity in this variety! Whether his brow was clouded with deepest care or the light of unruffled calmness glistened in his eye, in the kind-hearted tenderness or the severe earnestness of his language he was always the *same* identical Luther—"Luther entirely as Luther"—the man cast from one mould, the thoroughly original *character*, glorified by the divine lustre of faith, and borne up and pervaded by the Spirit of God. Thus Luther appears in Coburg.

But before we turn to Luther in Coburg during the meeting of the Diet, we must give a brief narrative of the state of the times and of the preparations for the Diet, including Luther's journey to that place.

At the end of the year 1529 and the beginning of 1530, Protestantism was in a very depressed and perilous condition.

Charles V. had secured peace in all countries either by force of arms or by diplomacy. His difficulties with Italy were happily adjusted by the Peace of Cambray in August, 1529. The hands of Francis I. of France were tied, and for the present he was rendered powerless to prosecute any warlike enterprise against the emperor in Spain, in the Netherlands or on the Rhine. In vain had the

Turks under Sultan Soliman besieged Vienna from the 26th of September to the 14th of October, 1529, and they were driven back to Hungary. With Pope Clement VII., Charles had concluded a peace on June 29, 1529.

In Bologna the emperor and pope, since November 5, 1529, had occupied two adjoining houses, which were united by a door through the interior, and both rulers had keys which unlocked it. In immediate and undisturbed intercourse with each other, all their former differences were adjusted and all their measures of Church and State against the Protestants were here secretly concocted. How could circumstances have been more favorable to turn the religious affairs of Germany to the advantage of the empire and of popery! Yet there was danger in delay. The evangelical States had assumed a positive stand at Speyer on April 19, 1529, and their meetings in Saalfeld, Rotach, Schlaiz, Swabach and Schmalkald, toward the end of the year and in the beginning of 1530, betokened a combination of efforts and of interests.

Under these circumstances, Charles hastened to adopt measures adapted to settle the religious difficulties which existed, and which threatened the peace of the empire and the unity of the Church. In the Peace of Barcelona he obligated himself to make another peaceable attempt immediately to bring back the recusants to the bosom of the Romish Church; but if this measure did not succeed, then he would employ force "to avenge the dishonor that had been heaped on Christ."

To this end, on January 21, 1530, at Bologna, he proclaimed an imperial DIET to meet at Augsburg. Against an *œcumenical Church council* on German soil, Pope Clement had prudently protested, fearing that too many equitable demands would be made of the Church. The Diet was appointed for the 8th of June. The emperor declared his intention to be personally present, and ordered the princes also to appear. The proclamation breathed the most peaceful sentiments. The most important subjects which were to be considered were averting the *dangers threatened by the Turks* and deciding the *religious controversies* which distracted the people. In reference to the latter, it was expressly promised that the question should be, " How shall the divisions and disputes concerning the holy faith and the Christian religion be treated and decided?" "It is the desire of the emperor," says the proclamation, "to heal the divisions, to submit past errors to our Saviour, and, further, *patiently and kindly to hear and consider every opinion, sentiment and counsel*, so that Christian truth may be elicited, and to lay aside everything which both parties may not agree upon, so that they may adopt the one 'only true religion, to live together in one communion, Church and Christian unity, and in common to establish and maintain harmony and peace.'" A more favorable and generous proposition Charles could not have made to the evangelical representatives of the states. He herein expressed their own wishes distinctly. If the intentions of the emperor had been honestly carried out, the result of the Diet would have been entirely different.

John the Constant, elector of Saxony since 1525, was, with the landgrave Philip of Hessen, at the head of the Protestant party. He received the proclamation on Friday, March 11. Opinions were divided at the electoral court upon the design of the emperor. Some of the counsellors of the elector regarded the mildness of the call as a sham for the purpose of enticing the evangelical princes to Augsburg that they might be personally seized, if necessary. They advised the elector not to appear in Augsburg. Others, among them the electoral prince John Frederick and Chancellor Brück, also called Pontianus, were of a different opinion, which determined the decision of the elector. In a letter to the emperor, Wednesday, March 23, he said: "Agreeably to the proclamation of your Imperial Majesty, I have determined, as far as God the Almighty grants me health, to be present at your proposed Diet." At the same time, he congratulated the emperor upon his coronation, of which he had received notice the day before. This occurred at Bologna on Feb. 24, 1530, the thirtieth birthday of Charles, by the hand of the pope. At former coronations the electors were invited to attend, and German knights formed the escort. Philip of the Palatinate was the only German prince present, and he was without official dignity on the occasion, and Antonio de Seiva, a *Spaniard*, commanded the *German* soldiers. Not *Germany*, then but *Spain* and *Italy* were the witnesses of this coronation of a *German* emperor. This was evidence enough of the deep chasm between the emperor and the empire. A wide and profound abyss on account of the gospel was opened in Germany, and divided it into a Catholic majority and a Protestant minority.

Above all things, it was now the interest of the elector of Saxony to establish a safe *scriptural* basis for the ensuing religious negotiations, and to arm himself with effective weapons for a possible conflict. At Speyer he with others had declared: "We have determined, with the grace and help of God, to adhere to that which alone is the word of God and the holy gospel as it is contained in the Old and New Testaments and which is purely preached, and to reject everything which opposes it. For therein, as the only true and proper guide of all Christian doctrine and conduct, no man can err; and he who builds thereon will be secure against the gates of hell, and before which all human inventions must fall." To this principle John *the Constant* desired to be faithful at Augsburg, and in accordance with it he would judge the imperial proposition for union. Everything which agreed with it was in advance sanctioned by his conscience, and that which was contrary to it was already rejected.

In preparation of this emergency, he informed his Wittembergen theologians, Luther, Melanchthon, Jonas and Bugenhagen, of the invitation of the emperor and of the design of the Diet, and requested them to prepare a summary of "all the articles in dispute concerning the faith and other external Church usages," so that before the opening of the Diet he might fully make up his mind "how and to what extent he and other States who have adopted the true faith could properly and conscientiously negotiate upon these subjects without oppressive vexation on the part of the opponents." The theologians were ordered to lay aside all other work, and personally to appear before him at Torgau, at the latest on March 20, with the result of their consultation.

When the electoral summons arrived at Wittenberg, Jonas was absent on a tour of visitation. Luther wrote to him to return immediately, but, not even waiting for him, the three others present began the task. The "Swabach Articles," which Luther had previously prepared for the meeting of the evangelical States and princes at Swabach (October, 1529), were adopted as the basis. On March 20, agreeably to the order, the four theologians appeared at Torgau and laid before the elector the Articles, seventeen in number, for examination and acceptance. From the place of their delivery, they were called "The Torgau Articles." Against Luther's will, they were soon made public, and were violently attacked by several theologians of the electorate of Brandenburg. Subsequently, at Coburg, Luther vindicated them in a pamphlet entitled *Martin Luther's Reply to the Screams of several Papists over the Seventeen Articles.* From these originated the "Augsburg Confession" by the hands of Melanchthon. They contained a brief summary of the opinions of the evangelical party upon God, redemption, sin, Church sacraments, ordination, etc., but the principal doctrine was justification by faith.

Thus was the first and most important preparation made for the tour to Augsburg.

Among other measures, mostly of a secular and administrative character, one is specially worthy of notice. An order was issued, that during the session in Augsburg prayer was to be offered in all the pulpits of the electorate for a happy issue of the Diet. In relation to the retinue of the elector, it was determined that, besides Melanchthon, Jonas and the court-preacher, Spalatin, Luther should also accompany the elector, but that until further notice Luther was to remain at Coburg.

It is very evident why his electoral protector did not take him with him to the Diet. Luther was yet under the ban of the edict of Worms (May, 1521). It was thought that being absent he could be of more service as an adviser, and that being present his impulsive and independent nature might perhaps disturb the even course of things. It is very evident why Coburg was selected as the place of Luther's residence. It was situated within the electoral territory; it afforded perfect security and isolation, and, from its proximity to Augsburg, facilitated frequent intercourse between him and that city.

It was, plainly, hard for the fiery spirit of

Luther to submit to this measure. His very first letter to his friend Nicolaus Hausman, minister in Zwickau, gives evidence of his discontent. Although sufficiently aware of the motives, he still says: "The prince has ordered me to remain at Coburg whilst the others go to the Diet: I do not know why." Still more ardently did the flame of his impatience gradually burn on account of the subtlety of the opponents in Augsburg and the timidity of Melanchthon and of his theological friends. If it had been left to him, he would have hastened to Augsburg on the wings of the wind, and, as in Worms, he would have stood up before emperor, princes and prelates, and have thrown the weight of his powerful word and presence in the scale of the decision on the fate of the gospel he so ardently loved.

All this will appear more distinctly from his letters to be quoted hereafter. We will only add here what he wrote, on the Saturday evening before his departure from Wittenberg, to his friend in Zwickau and his colleague Conrad Cordatus, upon the ensuing journey: "I am going with the prince as far as Coburg, and at the same time with Philip and Jonas, until we know how things are going on at Augsburg. But you must take pains to have your church heartily pray for the Diet. Farewell in the grace of Christ, and remember me in your supplications." The letter to Cordatus concludes with this observation: "I hear that you are anxious to be present at the Diet. This I cannot advise. First, because I am not called to it, but that I am to accompany the prince only on the way within his territory, for certain reasons. Second, because I do not believe that anything will be done there in the work of the gospel, for the princes are not so zealous for the gospel, but will rather consult about the affair of the Turks. Be content for the present; you will get there at the proper time."

It is evident from this that Luther had little hope of the adjustment of the religious difficulties by the Diet. But it turned out better than he feared. The providence of God, the resolution of the Protestant princes and States, and the influence of Luther itself claimed the triumph of evangelical truth in the conflict with the emperor Charles and his spiritual and secular confederates. The Diet at Augsburg and Luther's residence at Coburg constitute the radiant point in the first development period of the Protestant Church. Subsequent memorials growing out of this momentous era are only separated rays of that sun, and can hence cast but a feeble glimmer upon those heroes who in Coburg and Augsburg, clothed with the panoply of faith and armed with the sword of the divine word, contended against human inventions and abuses in the Church.

On Sunday, April 3, Luther preached in Torgau, in the presence of the electoral court, upon the words of Jesus (Matt. x. 32): "He that confesseth me before men, him will I confess before my heavenly Father."

The courage of the faithful confessor of Christ, the aged elector John, was strengthened by this sermon in the great purpose of bearing testimony to the pure gospel in Augsburg before the emperor and the realm. Immediately after, he set out upon his journey, accompanied by his son, the electoral prince John Frederick, at that time twenty-seven years old, and with a numerous retinue.

Besides Luther, Melanchthon and Jonas,

there belonged to this retinue of princes, dukes and knights Prince Wolfgang of Anhalt, Duke Franz of Luneburg, the counts Albert and Jobst of Mansfeld, Duke Ernst of Gleichen and Lord von Windelfels; of the electoral counsellors, there were Sebastian and Joachim Marschall von Pappenheim, Hans von Minckwitz, Frederick von Thun, Hans von Weissenbach, Kunz Goszman and Ewald von Brandenstein; also the two chancellors Dr. Brück and Dr. Baier. Besides these, there were seventy noblemen with about one hundred and sixty mounted servants, all armed with guns and clothed in brown-colored costume. As a theological counsellor, Duke Albert of Mansfeld took M. John Agricola of Eisleben with him. At Altenberg the electoral court-preacher, Spalatin, was to join the retinue as secretary of the elector. The elector John had sent his court-marshal, Hans von Dolzigk, in advance to the imperial headquarters. He was commissioned to treat with the two counsellors of the emperor, the dukes of Weimar and Nassau, concerning the investiture of the elector, as well as the confirmation of the marriage contract of John Frederick with Sybilla of Cleve and Iulich. Both of these demands the emperor had hitherto refused. This refusal was founded on Charles's displeasure at the elector and his son for favoring "the new doctrine." Both were made to feel the weight of the imperial dissatisfaction. By continuing this refusal, Charles hoped yet in Augsburg to shake the firmness of these men, hitherto so constant in the faith. ' The result convinced him, however, that Christian fidelity and conscientiousness could not be bought by worldly advantage.

The journey of the elector and his retinue from Torgau to Coburg, with various delays, consumed nearly fourteen days. They spent the first night at Grimma. On Wednesday, April 6, John delayed in Altenberg, from which place Spalatin joined the suite. On Saturday, the 9th, they arrived at Weimar. The next day, Palm Sunday, the elector, with John Frederick, Franz von Luneberg and others of his distinguished attendants, partook of the Lord's Supper in both kinds (bread and wine) in the city church. On this occasion, and at other times during their sojourn in Weimar, Luther preached. At various other places during the journey he was called on to perform the same service. Finally, on the 16th, the Saturday before Easter, they reached Coburg. Here the elector waited to receive authentic information of the place where the emperor then was, and of his arrival in Augsburg. For at that time only so much was known, that the emperor had left Bologna on February 22, and intended to remain for some time in Mantua. From this it is evident that the emperor was in no hurry to reach Augsburg. But it was soon enough discerned that he purposely delayed, in order thereby to accomplish his design. How far he succeeded will be made evident from the subsequent narrative.

CHAPTER II.

FROM THE ARRIVAL OF LUTHER AT COBURG TO THE ENTRANCE OF THE ELECTOR JOHN OF SAXONY INTO AUGSBURG.
(April 16 to May 2, 1530.)

THUS, then, Luther was in Coburg, where, at the command of the elector, a chamber looking south, in the second story of the well-guarded ancient castle, was assigned to him for his residence. He had been there before, when, in the spring of 1518, he travelled to Heidelberg to the meeting of the Augustinian order. How much had occurred in the mean time, and what changes had taken place! He had also since that time consulted with the Coburgers about their Church reforms in 1525. What an imposing and instructive picture full of the freshness of life is gradually unfolded to our view when we linger near him in his solitude and see him in constant intercourse with the

Diet at Augsburg, until his departure, at the beginning of October!

It will be appropriate at this place to present the general characteristics of this picture in an outline sketch.

Here, in Coburg, Luther labored, prayed and counselled for half a year. During this time the Protestant princes, in connection with the evangelical cities and the greatest theologians of the day on the one side, and the emperor, kings, dukes, lords, knights and other influential opponents of the Reformation on the other, surrounded with all the glory of the Church and the realm, in the midst of an assembly such as Germany had not seen before nor since, were exhibiting the remarkable spectacle of a spiritual combat for and against the liberty of the gospel and of conscience. From his chamber in this ancient abode of princes and electors, invisible as the soul is to the body, Luther guided with the magnetic force of his spirit the friends of the gospel at Augsburg. He is the counsellor, comforter, leader of princes and theologians, the marshal of the warriors fighting for God and Christ with the sword of the gospel. Nothing was done on the part of the elector and his theologians without first having heard Luther's opinion. The eyes and ears of the Protestant participants in these transactions were turned to Luther.

In the midst of all this he was untiringly active in the cause of the gospel in another sphere, and he sent forth a large number of his immortal writings. The most important of them, unquestionably, is his *Admonition to the Clergy Assembled at the Diet of Augsburg*, which had been sent to the press at Wittenberg early in May. This *Admonition* represents the ecclesiastical errors and abuses prevalent. They are powerfully set forth, and so full of faith and gospel Protestantism as to be well worthy of studious perusal by us of the present day. His *Letter to the Elector Albert of Mayence* (July 6), with the appended exposition of Ps. ii., and its application to the Diet and to the opposition of the mighty against the Lord and his anointed, is rich in thought and a living effusion of his devotion to Christ, and of his patriotic efforts against the malign influence of Rome over the Church and Germany. Quotations from both these writings shall be given at the appropriate place. He also wrote at Coburg his admirable *Sermon on the Education of Young Persons*, the satirical *Echo from Purgatory*, a treatise *On the Keys* (the power of the Church to forgive and to retain sin) *and Justification*, an *Extract from the Book on Monastic Vows, Forty Latin Discourses on the Power of the Church, Admonition to the Sacrament of the Body and Blood of Christ*, and a most excellent treatise on the qualifications of a translator of the Holy Scriptures with the title *Letter on Translation, Thoughts on Private Mass, Answer to the Questions of two Persons of High Rank on Monastic Life and the Mass*, and many others.

And yet all this is but a portion of the labors which the gigantic industry of Luther, with pen in hand, performed, during his sojourn at Coburg, in the service of the evangelical Church. The translation of the Bible which he had begun on the Wartburg, and continued through the year 1521, was nearly finished at Coburg.

He not only received a large number of *documents* from various places, which were to be read and answered, but he wrote also, including these replies, so many letters that it is really wonderful how the time and strength of one man could endure to satisfy these numerous demands. Many of these longer letters are lost, and yet, in De Wette's *Collection of Luther's Letters* (four volumes, 8vo), one hundred and nineteen were written at Coburg. Some of them bear the date "From the Kingdom of Birds," "From the Assembly of the Daws," in playful allusion to the multitude of daws which nestled in the towers of the castle and kept up a constant din; others are dated "From Gruboc," an inversion of the word "Coburg;" others, "From the Desert," as nine years before, at Worms, to conceal the place of his residence; and in only a few is the real name given. At the advice of his electoral patron, he employed these measures of precaution so that he might not betray his residence to his enemies. If they had known where he was concealed, they would have attempted to abduct him. At the same time, he protected himself against those who felt a sympathetic interest in him, and who might have disturbed him by frequent well-intended visits, as was the case with some who had ascertained the place of his seclusion. Of these visits we shall speak at the proper time.

Most of these letters are directed to the elector John, to Melanchthon, Jonas, Spalatin and many other persons, and some to his "dear master Lady Katharine Luther in Wittenberg." They all "breathe"—as Planck says, in contrast with the timidity of Melanchthon and of the other theologians in Augsburg—"that unterrified and cheerful courage which the weakest spirit cannot observe without admiration, and cannot admire without being fired and borne along with it." At the same time, some of these letters are full of incomparable wit, which shows that Luther, amid the perils for the gospel's sake which threatened him, and suffering severe bodily ailments, could yet, by unshaken confidence in God and prayer, maintain a serenity of spirit which astonishes us the more the less it could be expected; for at Coburg he also endured much physical suffering, as at Wartburg. He also suffered from sleeplessness, and several letters of Melanchthon to Luther's *famulus*, the industrious Veit Dietrich, are full of anxious inquiries concerning this evil. He also complains frequently of tormenting toothache and affections of the throat. But, above all, he was almost constantly troubled with ringing in his ears and vertigo, for which the elector, through his private physician, Dr. Caspar Linderman, sent him medicine.

He regularly attended the preaching of the castle chaplain, John Karg, often preached himself, frequently partook of the Lord's Supper, prayed diligently, amused himself with his lute and sang for his encouragement his celebrated hymn, most probably written here, "Ein' feste Burg ist unser Gott." To the same end he made a collection of beautiful and appropriate Scripture passages and wrote on the windows and doors certain mottoes, that he might have them always in view; such as: "I shall not die, but live and declare the works of the Lord;" "I shall lie down, and my sleep shall be sweet;" "The way of the ungodly shall perish." In order to sing them, he composed special tunes for them. Besides this, he found recreation in translating Æsop's Fables. Sometimes he descended from the castle into the town to visit the preacher John Lang and the knight Von Sternberg, and did not consider it beneath his dignity to amuse himself occasionally with shooting with the bow and arrow. He, however, refused an invitation to a wedding, and sent instead to the young bridal couple a salt-cellar in the shape of a stag, which contained a ducat, besides some instruction on three things which are experienced in married life—trouble and labor, joy and happiness, vexation and disappointment.

The numerous letters to his wife, his touching lamentations upon the death of his father, his sympathy with the joys and sorrows of his friends, his solicitude for the oppressed, his poetical, and yet simple, letters to his four-year-old son "Hänschen Luther," breathing all the overflowing affection of a tender father,—all these and many more of his acts present to us an interesting view of the inner life of this remarkable man.

In a word, "Luther," says Pfizer in his *Life of Martin Luther*—"Luther in Coburg is a stupendous event. He whom they feared to take with them to Augsburg, whom they carefully concealed—he, with unflinching boldness casting aside the veil of caution from himself, appeared upon the battle-field with the irresistible power of his pen, and whilst, during the strife, the men specially engaged therein on the spot occasionally wavered on account of indistinctness of view, and seemed to lose the advantage of cool reflection and to falter for lack of courage, he, elevated above the dust of the conflict, was called on to observe everything, to weigh, determine, cheer, warn and rebuke; and all this he did without presuming upon his superiority over all his co-workers: he did it in the consciousness of being led and strengthened by the Spirit of God, and by earnest prayer combining his activity with its proper source—the wisdom and power of God."

This "stupendous event" in Luther's life can be properly appreciated only by an examination of his writings and his extensive correspondence during his residence at this place in connection with the proceedings at Augsburg in all their particulars. Thus alone can we secure the *original likeness in life-size;*

but still, a *sketch on a reduced scale* will furnish us with traits of character which will excite our most profound admiration. Such a sketch alone have we room to present, and that shall be drawn from his writings and letters to various persons as they have been published. Besides these, it will be necessary to have constantly in view the progress of events at Augsburg. For, as the history of the Diet cannot be properly understood disconnected from the history of Luther in Coburg, so, on the other hand, does Luther in Coburg appear only in its proper light through the Diet at Augsburg. The history of the Diet forms the background and the accessories for the picture of Luther at Coburg. We shall therefore introduce all the events occurring there which will contribute to a full understanding and appreciation of the principal figure in our sketch.

As Luther had frequently preached while on the journey to Coburg, he continued to perform the same service during the sojourn of the elector with his retinue at that place.*

---

* All these sermons were published. See Kraft's Collection, etc.

Before the elector left, Luther wrote the following letter to his friend Hausman at Zwickau on April 18: "Grace and peace in Christ, my dear Hausman! I have spoken with Martin Saugner and told him everything, as he will inform you. Besides, please tell our Cordatus that we are still here in a state of inactivity, and do not know when we shall leave. Yesterday a messenger came with letters, from which we learn that the emperor still delays in Mantua and will spend Easter there. It is also said that the papists are employing all means to prevent the Diet, because they fear that measures injurious to their interests might be adopted. Further, that the pope is indignant at the emperor because the latter is mingling with spiritual affairs and wishing to join the party against the pope; for he had fondly thought the emperor would be only his constable against the heretics, and bring back everything to the old condition. For they will change nothing and yield nothing; nor will they consent to an investigation, but only that we shall be judged and condemned and they restored to their former state. But thus they will be put down and utterly come to naught. The ungodly must be blinded when they are destined to destruction. Some of them even believe that the Diet will fail, and that nothing will come out of it. The prince has ordered me to remain at Coburg whilst the rest go to the Diet. I do not know why. Thus everything is very uncertain from one day to the other."

According to this letter, news came to Coburg that the emperor was sojourning in Mantua, where he had already been for some time. Besides this, the elector received a letter from the emperor, dated at Mantua, April 8. In it he excuses the postponement of his arrival in Augsburg on the ground of his coronation and the necessary adjustment of Italian affairs. As soon as the latter were settled, he (the emperor) would hasten to Augsburg by way of Innspruck, and would there give counsel concerning "the duties and affairs of the German people," as it was stated in the proclamation of the Diet. If the elector should not yet be on the way, "he need not start on the journey, but make such arrangements to be in Augsburg at the end of this month." He himself, "God willing," would personally appear at that time.

This was the state of things when, on Friday after Easter, April 22, the elector John left Coburg and proceeded toward Augsburg by way of Bamberg and Nurnberg. The scene must have been very impressive when the elector himself, the electoral prince and all the retinue—among them Melanchthon, Jonas, Bugenhagen, Spalatin—took leave of Luther. Uncertain of the results of the Diet and of the time when or whether they would ever see each other again, no doubt painful anxiety was expressed upon their countenances and many questions ominous of the future were asked.

We can easily conceive how solitary Luther must have felt when the last horse of the elector's retinue passed out of sight, and when he was left alone in the castle with no one but his devoted amanuensis Veit Dietrich and his faithful servant Cyriac. This sensation of loneliness is sufficiently revealed in letters to Melanchthon and Jonas, written on the very day of their departure.

To Melanchthon he says: "We have finally reached our Sinai, my dearest Philip, but we will make a Zion out of this Sinai and here build three tabernacles—one to the Psalter, one to the Prophets and one to Æsop; but this last one is a worldly affair. The place is indeed a very pleasant one and favorable to study; only your absence makes it sad. I am beginning to be extremely indignant at the Turks and Mahomet, because I must be a witness of that intolerable raging of Satan against body and soul. Hence I will most fervently pray until my cry shall be heard in heaven. . . . I pray Christ to grant you refreshing sleep, and that you may be delivered from painful anxieties—that is, from the fiery darts of Satan. Amen! I am writing this for pastime, for I have not yet received my chest containing my papers and other things, nor have I yet seen either of the two castellans. In other respects nothing is wanting in my solitary residence. The large wing projecting from the castle has been prepared for me, and I have the keys to all the apartments. I am told that more than thirty men are kept here, of whom twelve guard the castle at night and two are posted on each tower.

But why should I mention this? Only because I have nothing else to say. Salute Doctor Caspar and Magister Spalatin, etc. From the Kingdom of Birds, 3 o'clock, April 22, 1530.—MARTINUS LUTHER, D."

And yet how cheerful he could be under these circumstances, and how playfully he could write, abundantly appears from a letter to Justus Jonas of the same date.

The same matter, though presented in a more lively style, he communicates to his "table companions" at Wittenberg, and on May 9 he wrote a similar letter to Spalatin. We shall here quote the one to his friends at Wittenberg:

"Grace and peace in Christ! Dear sirs and friends, I have received your joint letters and properly considered them. That you may know the state of things here, I will say that I, Master Veit and Cyriac are not going to the Diet at Augsburg, but we are attending another Diet of a quite different character.

"There is just under our window a small grove, in which the jackdaws and the rooks have opened a Diet. There is such a riding to and fro, such an incessant cawing day and night, as if they were all thoroughly, crazily drunk; young and old cackle among each other at such a rate that I wonder how their voice and breath can hold out so long. I should like to know whether any representatives of this nobility and knight-errantry company have thus far appeared among you; for it seems to me as if they had assembled here from all ends of the world.

"I have not yet seen their emperor, but their nobles and heads of great families float and expand their tails constantly before our eyes. They are not, indeed, sumptuously clothed, but simply and in one color—all alike black and all alike gray-eyed. They all sing the same song in the same tune, but with a pleasing difference of pitch between the young and the old, the little and the big. They do not envy the palaces and halls of the great, for their hall is arched by the wide and beautiful heavens, their floor is the broad field, and wainscoted with green, flourishing foliage and flowers, and the walls extend to the ends of the earth. Neither are they solicitous about horses and carriages: they have winged wheels, by which they escape from the rifle and rouse the wrath of the sportsman. They are great and mighty lords, but I do not yet know what subjects they are discussing.

"As far as I have learned from an interpreter, they are carrying on a tremendous fight against wheat, barley, oats, and all species of grain, and many great knights in this war will perform mighty deeds.

"Thus we take our seats in the Diet and hear with great pleasure how the princes and lords and other states of the empire joyfully sing and caress each other. But it gives us particular pleasure to see the knightly dignity with which they waggle their tails, wipe their bills, stretch out their necks, as if they had acquired honor in their attack upon corn and malt. We wish them all happiness, and that they all may be impaled upon one fence-rail.

"But I hold that these are nothing else than the sophists and papists, with their sermons and writings. These I must always have in view, hearing their pleasing voices and observing what a useful folk it is in consuming everything on earth and cackling for the whole world. M. L."*

On May 2, four weeks after the departure from Torgau, the elector, with his retinue, was in sight of the towers of Augsburg. An immense concourse of people had gathered when he, the first of all the princes, who gradually arrived, made his entrance into the city. One hundred and sixty of his retinue were mounted on splendidly-caparisoned horses, and each man was armed. The baggage-wagons were drawn by one hundred horses besides.

The elector remained in Augsburg from

---

* This "grove" in which the council of jackdaws and crows was held is at the present time supplanted by a vineyard and fruit-orchard. But in the immediate vicinity of the fortress there still stand some ancient trees, upon which the imperial deputies (the daws and crows) which so deeply interested the Reverend Martin still hold their meetings and make wonderful speeches.

During the Thirty Years' War some of Luther's relics were sacrificed. Some mottoes in his handwriting are still preserved in an old ruined church in the neighborhood, but their authenticity cannot be assured. A bed of Luther's is still shown, also a table which is said to have been his. A number of vessels of Luther's *time* are also exhibited, but none which he himself *used* are extant at that place.

May 2 to September 23, and his quarters were the meeting-place of all the evangelical sympathizers with the Diet, and the point—as it were, a fountain—from which proceeded all the heroic deeds of faith which were enacted in that city.

CHAPTER III.

FROM THE ARRIVAL OF ELECTOR JOHN OF SAXONY TO THE ENTRANCE OF THE EMPEROR CHARLES V.

(MAY 2 TO JUNE 18, 1530.)

THE Diet of Augsburg was the theatre of momentous proceedings concerning faith and conscience, and its grand results aided a large portion of Christendom in securing and preserving the most sacred possessions. Its history shows, even to the present day, how immensely important to the interests of the Protestant Church was the arrival of the elector John of Saxony on May 2, 1530. This event opened the barriers to the ensuing contest for the prize of victory between the papal powers and the civil despotism on the one hand, and the gospel on the other. The 2d of May gave the first signal for the beginning of the world-historical spectacle which was exhibited to the eyes of mankind by the emperor and the States.

It was of special interest and importance that the elector of Saxony should be the first of all the princes to arrive. Next to the emperor, he was the most potent and influential among the German princes of his time, and the most esteemed among the evangelical States of the empire. His appearance on the spot displayed his earnest obedience to the head of the realm, and his early arrival bore unequivocal evidence of his heroism in the decisive hour. The astonishment which his advent in Augsburg occasioned his opponents shows the extent of the peril to which he had exposed himself and the responsibility he had assumed. The fact of his bringing with him a company of such distinguished theologians also showed to all, the nature of the purpose which he had in view. The word of God, above all, was the weapon with which these theologians, with Melanchthon in Augsburg and Luther at Coburg at their head, were armed, and which the Spirit of God qualified them to wield with terrible energy against all unevangelical doctrines and customs.

One circumstance especially displays the ruling of divine Providence in this early appearance of the elector in connection with the retarded arrival of the emperor. Slowly the latter pursued his journey from Mantua to Trient, Innspruck and Munich. In Innspruck he whiled away the time from May 4 to June 6, and it was only on June 15—the evening before the festival of Corpus Christi, six weeks later than the elector—that he celebrated his magnificent entrance into Augsburg. His design was very evident: it was to embarrass the Protestant princes by an order to take part in the procession of the festival of Corpus Christi, and thus to put their unity and firmness to a very dangerous test. The painful waiting from week to week was in itself, irrespective of the great expense which it occasioned, calculated to exhaust the patience of the princes, and even to disgust them with the unnecessarily protracted arrival of the emperor and the consequent postponement of the Diet. The expense of living increased just in proportion as the princes, with their large retinues, and the deputies arrived. The elector John alone paid over two thousand guilders a week for his maintenance, which was a large sum for those times. The emperor was aware of all this, and presumed that these men would be willing to do anything to gratify him if he would only open the Diet and proceed to business.

But their firmness and perseverance far exceeded the hopes of the emperor; and as since the time of Joseph it has often been realized in the history of the kingdom of God, "But as for you, ye thought evil against me, but God meant it unto good;" so it was in this case.

In the mean time, the princely opponents of the Reformation—as the elector Joachim I. of Brandenburg, Duke George of Saxony and Duke William of Bavaria—hastened to the emperor at Innspruck and cunningly hinted to him that the elector John was devising dangerous plans. An irreparable loss also occurred to the Protestants in this interim. The only one of the counsellors of the emperor who cherished feelings favorable to the Protestants, and which he would have brought with him to Augsburg, was his chancellor, the venerable cardinal Mercurinus Gattinara. Melanchthon's letters from Augsburg are full of praise of this great statesman. He thus writes to Luther, May 22, upon the different opinions which contended for supremacy with the emperor at Innspruck relative to proceedings against the Protestants: "There are two opposing views among the imperial counsellors. One party maintains that without further ceremony he should condemn our cause by an edict; the other holds that he should carefully investigate it and reform the abuses in the Church. To this latter party belongs the arch-chancellor Mercurinus, a man equally eminent as moderate, of whom it is said that, in spite of his infirm health, he followed the emperor in the hope that through his influence the affairs of the Church might be regulated in a becoming manner. He declared that he would not sanction any measures of force. He is reported to have said, 'In Worms it was evident that forcible measures do not accomplish the design.' For he was in the retinue and counsel of the emperor already at Worms."

Thus far Melanchthon; but at the very moment when the emperor intended to leave Innspruck for Augsburg, and when he most needed such a Gamaliel, Mercurinus died, at

Innspruck, on June 4, and by his death Bishop Waltkirchen of Constance, greatly to the disadvantage of the Protestants, secured the preponderance in the counsel of the emperor, who, for himself, was not disinclined to peaceable measures.

· Though these disadvantages weighed heavily against the Protestants, yet, on the other hand, the gain which the long absence of Charles secured to the princes and their theologians—and among them to Luther also—was great. They gained time for counsel and action in the unobstructed promotion of their holy designs. This will be manifest when we come to consider the occurrences of the six weeks between the arrival of the elector and that of the emperor. The facts of the case and the letters of the various characters concerned will distinctly illustrate this point. They will also fully exhibit the unshaken confidence in God and the evangelical spirit of the men, and, above all, that of Luther.

In reference to the personal affairs and activity of Luther, we must in advance remark that the death of his father occurred at this time. He died at Mansfeld on May 29. The letters of Luther to Link and Melanchthon relative to this event are affecting evidences of the filial reverence and love which the great Reformer, in the height of his fame, still cherished for his father. They are remarkable contributions to the confirmation of the fact that he was both Christian and man, in the most exalted sense of the words.

To the same period belongs the finishing of *The Admonition to the Clergy*. The manuscript had been sent to the press at Wittenberg on May 12; in the beginning of June it was ready for publication, and on June 11 the electoral prince John Frederick sent copies to Innspruck to the court marshal Von Dolzigk, who was to distribute them among well-disposed men. For some time they were publicly sold at the residence of the elector, but subsequently the sale was prohibited upon the complaints of the opponents.

In the mean time, Luther's activity was frequently interrupted by severe attacks of sickness, and also occasionally by very agreeable visits. One of the most agreeable was that of a noble lady named Argula von Grumbach.

She was one of the warmest admirers of Luther—cherished and maintained his persecuted followers, wrote herself against the University of Ingolstadt and exhorted various princes to firmness in the Protestant doctrine. Jonas wrote to Luther concerning her, on June 25: "Good heavens! how much richer and better is Argula von Grumbach than all bishops who know not God and are not known of Him!"

The complaint, also, of Luther on the persevering silence of his friends at Augsburg for the time, is to be mentioned here. The intense longing for intelligence justified his complaint. The uncertainty of their condition, and their multiplied labors—especially Melanchthon's—explain their protracted silence. Besides this, letters were lost, and perhaps couriers were unfaithful.

But how otherwise than favorable to the cause of the gospel could that have been which occurred during the six weeks before the arrival of the emperor in Augsburg?

Immediately after the entrance of the elector John, he gratified the wishes of those citizens of Augsburg favorable to the gospel by ordering Agricola to preach in the church of the Dominicans as well as in St. Catharine's. In the latter the celebrated Urbanus Rhegius preached, who, as the result of that sermon, was called as superintendent to Celle by Duke Ernest of Brunswick. He was a correspondent of Luther at the beginning of the Diet, and on his tour to Celle he spent a whole day with him at Coburg, and thus writes: "On my way to Saxony, I spent a whole day with Luther, the man of God, and I have never had a more joyous time. No age has ever produced a more powerful theologian. I have always esteemed him most highly, but now my admiration of him is still greater; for I have seen and heard what no pen can describe. His books show the character of his mind and heart; but when you see him and hear him talk concerning divine things with the spirit of an apostle, you will say, 'It is true what people say, that Luther is a greater man than any faultfinder or sophist is able to appreciate.'"

Soon after, Philip, landgrave of Hesse, arrived at Augsburg with a retinue of one hundred and twenty horsemen. He also immediately established Protestant worship, and his court-chaplain, Schnepf, preached in the cathedral. Other distinguished men, such as Michael Kellner and others, performed similar services in other churches of the city, which were attended by crowds of persons disposed toward the gospel.

These sermons gave great offence to the opponents of the good cause, and it was not long before the fact was reported to the emperor at Innspruck. He immediately issued an order, through the electoral ambassador, Hans von Dolzigk, that this preaching should cease; and when the latter demurred, the emperor sent two of his counsellors, the counts Nuenar and Nassau, with secret instructions, to Augsburg, to carry his order into immediate effect. But in vain. In a letter to the imperial counsellors of May 31 the elector John repelled the accusations made, and in reference to the preaching expressed himself very decidedly: "As concerns the abandonment of the public worship here, we in all humility beg the Imperial Majesty not to compel us to order it, for we cannot do it with a good conscience, because our preachers teach nothing but the pure gospel and we do not allow them to mingle foreign and useless disputations with their sermons. For this reason it would be very oppressive if we were compelled to forbid them teaching the word of God and the plain truth. As all men are exposed to great and daily peril, against which there is no other help and consolation than the word of God, it would be very dangerous for us, in these times, to be deprived of the gospel. Inasmuch as we fear God and venerate His word, we cannot consent, with all due deference to his Majesty, that the preaching should be forbidden. Our preachers daily and diligently exhort the people to pray for the welfare of all Christendom, and especially that God would, in these perilous times, grant grace to his Majesty as the power ordained of Heaven, and to electors, princes and States of the empire, that all spiritual and worldly affairs may be so handled at this Diet as to promote the glory of God and universal peace and concord among men."

The letter proceeds to give various other reasons why the service should not be interrupted, and states the happy results of the preaching upon many hearers. It maintains that not a word has been uttered by the preachers that could offend any one desirous of knowing the truth; that "nothing seditious or blasphemous or unchristian or against the Catholic doctrine" has been taught. It deplores the melancholy consequences of prohibition, and in strong language shows that persistence in this purpose would be an evidence that the emperor had prejudged their cause and condemned their doctrine without a hearing.

This letter had its desired effect, and for the time the preaching was continued. But, as a formal prohibition was to be expected at the arrival of the emperor, the elector submitted the question not only to his theologians and counsellors in Augsburg, but also to Luther in Coburg, whether it was their duty as subjects to yield to such a prohibition, or whether they would be justified, on grounds of conscience, to disobey it. The opinion of the jurists, probably written by Chancellor Brück, most decidedly favored the continuance of the preaching, even in case of an imperial prohibition. But the theologians, at the head of whom stood Melanchthon, regarded the emperor as the civil lord of the imperial city, and were of the opinion that whilst they might remonstrate, yet that they were in duty bound to submit to his will if he forbade preaching, not only in the churches, but even in their own residences.

Luther also coincided in this opinion, and replied to the elector on May 15: "Concerning the question of submitting to the emperor, if he should desire your Grace to silence your preachers, my opinion is now, as formerly, that he is our master; the city and all are his, just precisely as we should not resist your Electoral Grace in Torgau, where you are master, if you should desire or order this or that to be done or to be let alone. Still, I should be pleased to see, if it were possible, that an attempt be made in all propriety and humility to change the mind of his Imperial Majesty, and that he should not forbid the preaching of the word unheard, but appoint some one to hear how we preach. The preaching of the pure, unadulterated word should not be forbidden, for we have not proclaimed anything in the least degree seditious or fanatical. If this will be of no service, we must let might prevail over right. We have done our duty, and are free from responsibility, etc."

In the same manner another question was settled. It was that concerning *eating meat* and *fast-days*. As a question indifferent, and which must be left to the decision of every man's conscience, it was concluded that in this also, concessions might be safely made. With the same unanimity, on the other hand, did the theologians, on scriptural grounds, resent the expected demand upon the evangelical States to attend the procession of Corpus Christi. These were measures and subjects for investigation and settlement of such manifest importance, that the continued absence of the emperor was advantageous in allowing more time for reflection.

This would also apply to the proceedings which could be transacted in the mean time relative to the indispensable *unity* in the Confession, on the part of the Wittenberg theologians and Luther, with the landgrave Philip. It is known that Philip leaned to the side of Zwingle on the doctrine of the Lord's Supper, and that he made zealous efforts to bring about a union between the Lutherans and the Sacramentarians, as Luther called the Swiss theologians. The colloquium which the landgrave instituted at Wartburg in 1529 had this object in view, but it did not succeed. He also continued these exertions at Augsburg, and was as anxious to accomplish the object as the elector John, who adhered to the true doctrine as taught by Luther, was strenuously opposed to it. The danger of division was great at that moment when unity was so desirable. For this reason, Melanchthon urged Luther to write to the landgrave to bring him over to the true faith and to warn him against fellowship with the Swiss. But before Melanchthon's letter reached Luther he had written one of his own suggestion, dated May 20. In this letter he argues the question vigorously and urges the landgrave to adopt the scriptural view; but it did not move him from his position, and he continued his unionistic efforts. Then Melanchthon, in connection with John Brantz, one of the most influential adherents of Luther and an imperial deputy to the council, wrote to the landgrave and endeavored to convince him of the unscriptural character of his exertions. Urbanus Rhegius also had a long interview with him, by invitation of the landgrave, and tried to convince him of his error. The result was that he subsequently signed the Augsburg Confession and became a powerful supporter of the cause. It may be asked whether this union of both sides would have occurred, if the emperor had not delayed his arrival so long, thus giving time for discussion and negotiation.

This is the proper place to allude to the most important subject connected with the further prosecution of the affairs of the Diet: it is the *Confession of Faith*, founded upon the Articles of Torgau, which was to be publicly delivered to the emperor. Already, in Coburg, Melanchthon, in consultation with Luther, had written an introduction to it, and on the way to Augsburg he had elaborated the Articles themselves. But the conscientious Melanchthon, upon further examination, was not satisfied with this first form of his *Apology*, as he at first called the Confession, nor with that amendment and corrected review of it which the elector had sent to Luther for examination on May 11, although Luther himself had expressed his entire approval of it in his reply of May 15. "I have," he writes to the elector—" I have read the *Apology* of M. Philip. It pleases me very much, and I do not find anything to improve or alter in it; neither would it become me to do it, for I could not treat the subject so gently. May Christ the Lord help to produce much and valuable fruit from it, as we hope and pray!" The Augsburg Confession was begun and finished in prayer.

Notwithstanding this approbation, Melanchthon continued to improve the Confession in matter and arrangement, as he reports to Luther on May 22: "I am daily improving the *Apology*. The Article on Vows was much too meagre; I have taken it out entirely and substituted one more extensive and thoroughly elaborated. At present I am working at 'The Office of the Keys.' I wish you had looked through the Articles on Faith; if they, in your judgment, were perfectly correct, I would treat all the rest just as I am now doing. Here and there they must be altered and adapted to circumstances."

If the Confession was subjected to such improvements until the moment of its delivery; if, irrespective of other consultations upon it, the "old chancellor Brück examined and amended it before and behind—*i. e.*, at the beginning and end;" and if it received the finished perfection in which we now glory,—we must even at the present day give thanks to the emperor Charles and his councillors, who, by protracting the meeting of the Diet, afforded the necessary time for the completion of this momentous document.

Before the arrival of the emperor in Augsburg the evangelical States, from all directions, had proceeded to that city, and the remaining princes and deputies gradually assembled when the emperor, with his brother, King Ferdinand, and Anna, the wife of the latter, and Maria, the widowed queen of Hungary —who was a sister of the emperor and personally acquainted with Luther—finally broke up their quarters at Innspruck on June 6.

On their way they were everywhere received with loyal demonstrations of various kinds. They tarried three days at Munich amid the most brilliant festivities, and on June 15 they advanced toward Augsburg.

It was after seven o'clock in the evening of this day that Charles—at that time thirty years and six months of age—mounted on a white stallion of Polish breed, with his numerous retinue of princes, prelates, vassals, pages, and domestics of Spanish, Flemish, Bohemian and German origin, arrived at the Lech bridge, a few miles from Augsburg. The electors, princes and prelates who had already assembled in the city rode out that distance with their retinue to meet him. The papal legate Campegi also saluted him and pronounced a blessing upon him. In addition, the city council, citizens and clergy of Augsburg had come out to greet him with every demonstration of honor, and, thus surrounded with all the glory of worldly majesty and ecclesiastical protection, he entered the city, first proceeding to the cathedral, where solemn high mass was celebrated, and then to his quarters in the episcopal palace. "This pageantry," it is reported, "continued until ten o'clock at night."

On this same evening the emperor urged upon the elector John, the margrave George of Brandenburg, the landgrave Philip and Duke Ernest of Lüneburg, the demand to prohibit preaching by their theologians, and to participate in the procession of Corpus Christi on the next day. But before we proceed to this matter it will be proper here to introduce a number of letters of the elector, of Luther and Melanchthon, which will in general serve to illustrate the purpose of our sketch *Luther in Coburg*. Besides other interesting particulars, we learn from them specially the active sympathy of the elector and Melanchthon in the condition of Luther's health, and how he reciprocated this sympathy.

Immediately upon his arrival at Augsburg, Melanchthon writes to Veit Dietrich, in Coburg, on May 4: "You did me a great favor by giving me an account of the doctor's condition, and of other matters. . . . I am much concerned about the state of his sore leg and his sleeplessness. You must take pains, by reciting stories and the use of other means, to prevent him from going to bed with his mind excited about the events of the day, although I well know that it is hard, by the use of human means, to tranquillize his mind when in a state of excitement. We shall, in the mean time, betake ourselves to prayer in his behalf.... If our Luther is restored to health, all will go well again. We have the best to hope from the Diet.... Probably I shall soon be with you, and bring with me the *Apology*, for examination, which is to be delivered to the emperor...."

Similar letters he frequently sent to Dietrich. To Luther himself he wrote, as mentioned before, on May 22: "We are all, including the elector, much concerned about your health. Hence we pray God that He would preserve you for the gospel's sake. We earnestly beg you to be careful about your health. Dr. Caspar has sent to you by the elector's messenger some medicines as tonics for your head and heart, for he loves you dearly."

Melanchthon's strong attachment to Luther moved him to write to his wife, Katharine, on the same day, and Jonas and Agricola also included a few lines of salutation. These men express the most tender interest in the lady and the profoundest sympathy in her during the absence of her husband, and write words of encouragement and cheer.

On May 8, Luther writes to Wenceslaus Link, in Nurnberg: "I am living here in peace and honor, and have begun to translate the remaining prophets, having finished Jeremiah. Perhaps I shall also publish several psalms, with an exposition; for I will not sit here idly. . . . I have also resolved to translate Æsop's Fables for the benefit of German youth. I know well enough how to employ my time. I must confess that I would like to be with you, but what pleases God also pleases me. I am of no use on this tour, and could perhaps have done more at home by teaching and counselling; but I could not resist the call. . . . I know nothing new from Wittenberg, except what Dr. Pommer* writes—that

---

* Bugenhagen.

the gospel is making good progress in Lübeck and Lüneburg, and that it is there openly and faithfully preached."

From a letter of Melanchthon to Luther of May 11 we make the following extracts: "Hereby you receive our *Apology*, although, more correctly, it is a *Confession;* for the emperor has no time to hear extensive discussions. I have said everything which, as I believe, is useful and suitable. . . . Duke George and Margrave Joachim have gone to Innspruck to see the emperor; they are there holding a Diet upon the subject of sparing our necks or not. . . . It is not at all doubted that the emperor will forbid the Zwinglian theologians from preaching. We presume that, under the same pretext, he will also forbid ours, as Eisleben* publicly preaches in the church. What is your opinion? Shall we yield when the emperor demands it? For my part, I have answered that we must submit to the will of the emperor, as we are guests in his city. But our old man" (it is not certain to whom Melanchthon here alludes)

---

* Another name for Agricola.

"is creating difficulties. I beg you to write your separate opinion on a sheet of paper."

Luther's approbation of the *Apology*, and his concurrence in opinion with Melanchthon on the subject of preaching in Augsburg, have already been expressed in his letter to the elector of May 15.

Luther had neglected to answer several of Melanchthon's letters, but on May 12 he wrote one from which we shall make a few extracts. After speaking of his engagements in translating the prophet Ezekiel he says: "But the outward old man is becoming very frail. I have felt a roaring in my ears not unlike thunderclaps; and if I had not ceased work immediately, I should have fainted, which I could scarcely avoid during two days together. To-day is the third day that I have not been able to read a single syllable. It cannot last long; the years are hastening on. . . . Gradually the ringing in my ears moderates, after I have used medicine. This is the reason why I have not answered your letters. The day on which yours from Nurnberg came, I had an embassy of evil spirits in my chamber. I was all alone, for Veit and Cyriac had gone away. Satan in so far gained the victory that he chased me out of my room and compelled me to go into company.

"But these are private affairs; in the outside world other events are occurring, which you report to me. It appears that Eck is beginning another controversy. What else is to be done at the Diet? The uncouth asses bray so much about the important affairs of our churches; but let them bray on and fail. Master Joachim (Camerarius) has sent me dry figs or dates or raisins, and has written twice in Greek; but I, when I shall have recovered, will answer him in Turkish, that he may have something to read which he does not understand. Why does he write Greek to me? I would write more, but I am afraid that I will provoke a new attack of headache. . . . I beg you, as well as all our friends, to be very careful of your health, and that you do not, as I have done, bring upon yourselves such attacks as I suffer. Do not become murderers of yourselves and then say that God would have it so. We also serve God by resting; . . . and hence he would have us observe the Sabbath so strictly. Do not throw this to the winds; I am writing to you the pure word of God."

During this correspondence Jonas lost his youngest son by death. Luther wrote to him a letter full of the tenderest sympathy, which he requested Melanchthon to forward to him.

In the same way he also expressed his condolence with his friend Link, in Nurnberg, upon the death of a young daughter.

The elector also felt the deepest interest in the condition of Luther's health, and wrote to him a letter replete with affectionate concern, and informing him that his own physician, Dr. Caspar, with the same messenger, had sent him medicine. This brought out from Luther a long letter of thanks, as well as of instruction and encouragement in view of the impending Diet; for the emperor had not yet at this time arrived at Augsburg.

In his letters of the first week in June to Melanchthon and Link, Luther speaks several times of the visits he received, of the silence of his friends at Augsburg concerning important matters, and of the death of his father. Among other things he says on June 2, 1530:

"Yesterday Hans Reynick of Mansfeld and George Römer, and to-day Argula von Stauffen, were here. As I see that these visits are becoming too frequent, I have determined, after the example of your Stromer, either to give out that I am not at home or go somewhere else for a day, so that the report may go abroad that I am no longer here. I beg of you so to speak and write in the future, so that nobody may come here to hunt me up. I want to be left alone and to keep your letters secret.

"We are told here that the Diet is retrograding, and will be at least postponed by the cunning and malevolence of the bishops until you shall have spent everything and be compelled to go home. It is doubted whether the elector of Trier and the Pfalz will go to the Diet. The emperor, who is entirely under the control of the papists, gives all sorts of excuses for his tardiness in not going to Augsburg."

In a letter of June 5 to Melanchthon he

complains bitterly of the neglect of his friends in Augsburg not writing to him as frequently as he thinks they should, and proceeds to say:

"We have heard that the emperor has commanded the Augsburgers to dismiss the mercenaries hired by them, and to remove the chains from the streets.* . . . To-day Hans Reynick writes that my dearly-beloved father died on May 29. This calamity has depressed me much; . . . and, although it is a source of consolation, as Reynick writes, that he died in the faith of the gospel, yet the event has deeply agitated me and cast a gloom over my whole soul. . . . I now enter upon the inheritance of the name, so that I am now almost become Luther Senior in my family."

On June 7 he writes:

"I see that you have all resolved to lacerate me by your silence, but, not to die unavenged, I hereby give you notice that I will rival you in silence; and if it is of no consequence to you what I do, I will praise my Wittenbergers, who write to me three times a

---

* The city authorities, in apprehension of a riot, had, as was the manner of that day, hired men to defend the city, and had stretched chains across the streets as barricades.

week on business matters, to your once. . . .
But I must here stop, not to give you occasion to be silent on account of my much scribbling.

"My wife writes me that the Elbe has again risen high, although there has been no rain. High water is a prognostic of a great calamity."

We will take this occasion to say in relation to the *visits* several times alluded to that, besides Argula von Stauffen, Urbanus Rhegius, Hans Reynicke and George Römer, the following-named persons also visited him during this period: The merchant Cyriacus of Mansfeld, his sister's son; his brother Jacob; Caspar Müller, a counsellor of Mansfeld; Peter Weller, a legal friend of his from Wittenberg; Caspar Aquila of Saalfeld; and the celebrated Martin Bucer, whose visit will be spoken of hereafter. These few persons of distinction alone are here mentioned. Besides these, there was a large number of idlers and curious people, who exceedingly annoyed him.

This is the proper place to mention *The Admonition to the Clergy*, which he wrote at Coburg. After an introduction, it treats, in eleven chapters, 1. Indulgence; 2. The Confessional; 3. Absolution; 4. Repentance; 5. Private or Mercenary Masses; 6. The Ban; 7. The Form of the Sacrament; 8. The Celibacy of the Clergy; 9. Church Discipline, Doctrine and Government; 10. Ancient Church Ceremonies; 11. Fasting. The treatise is written in his usual pungent style, exhibiting the truth in all simplicity and exposing the errors of the Church with terrible severity.

Amid such labors, experience and intercourse he spent at Coburg the eight weeks which elapsed between the departure from that place of the elector and the arrival of the emperor in Augsburg—truly a long time, considering the intense anxiety with which Luther anticipated coming events. It was nothing but his uninterrupted activity, as he himself tells us, that seemed to shorten the tiresome period.

CHAPTER IV.

FROM THE ENTRANCE OF THE EMPEROR CHARLES INTO AUGSBURG TO THE FIRST TRANSACTIONS OF THE OPPONENTS CON-CERNING THE AUGSBURG CONFESSION.

(FROM THE 15th TO THE 30th OF JUNE, 1530.)

AS the arrival of the elector of Saxony in Augsburg on May 2 was the first sign of the beginning of the great spectacle, so the entrance of the emperor was the rolling up of the curtain. The prelude, however, endured from the evening of June 15 to the 24th, the day of the delivery and reading of the Augsburg Confession. Particularly important during this time were the events occurring from the evening of the 15th to the 20th of June.

When the emperor, after the high mass in the cathedral, had repaired to the episcopal palace, and the other members of his retinue had ridden to their quarters, he detained the elector John, the landgrave Philip, the margrave George of Brandenburg and Duke Ernest of Lüneburg, and, as he was not sufficiently familiar with the German language, he through his brother Ferdinand strenuously insisted upon their prohibition of preaching, and upon their participation in the procession of Corpus Christi, on the following day. They promptly rejected both propositions with a resoluteness that was remarkable. The valiant margrave George upon the spot replied in the well-known words, "Before I consent to be deprived of the word of God and deny Him, I would kneel down and allow my head to be cut off."

The emperor, who caught the meaning of these words from the motion of the margrave's hand across his neck, replied, in his Low Netherland dialect, "Dear prince, not head off, not head off!"

Similar courage was displayed by the landgrave Philip. When Ferdinand said that the emperor would not permit any preaching, he replied, "His Imperial Majesty is not lord and master of men's consciences."

It was in vain that the emperor again summoned the elector to him at eleven o'clock at night; he excused himself by saying he was compelled to seek rest. It was in vain also that in an interview of three hours next morning he urged the evangelical princes to comply with his request, and through the Pfalzgrave Frederick he admonished them "that just as their forefathers, as pious Christian princes, did, so they also should uphold this act of worship and appear in the procession." Upon this the margrave George first replied in the name of his fellow-believers, and then in his own name. He again based his remarks on the word, alluded to his constant submission to the house of Austria and promised obedience in all things, but assumed that the gospel must be left untrammelled for him.

The procession of Corpus Christi was conducted with great pomp through the streets to the cathedral, the emperor himself carrying a burning taper. But no elector of Saxony preceded the emperor with a drawn sword, as was usual on such occasions; none of the other evangelical States participated in it. Even of the citizens of Augsburg, scarcely one hundred joined it. To that extent had the times changed. In regard to the preaching the Protestant Christians were to present their objections in writing. This was done on the next Friday, June 17, "before breakfast," in the provost's apartment of the cathedral. The princes based their opposition to suspend preaching upon the ground that their preachers taught the pure gospel as it was held and preached by the Fathers and accepted by the Christian Church in the purest times, and allowed also by the Diet at Nurnberg in 1523. They argued the whole subject at length, and vigorously maintained their civil and religious right to have the pure gospel preached to them by their own divines.

The answer was the subject of a whole day's deliberation by the other spiritual and civil dignitaries in the presence of the emperor; and, as no harmonious result was reached, the further consideration of the matter was referred to a committee composed entirely of opponents of gospel-preaching. Unconcerned about it, and even against the advice of the elector, the margrave George allowed his court-preacher, John Rurer, to preach on that day in St. Catharine's church. The reports inform us that an immense crowd of people attended the service.

On Saturday, June 18, the agreement was arrived at to suspend the preaching on both sides. The emperor alone was to "have the power of appointing preachers, who were, however, to preach nothing but the pure gospel."

In consequence of this, on the same evening, an imperial herald, amid a flourish of trumpets, rode through the streets proclaiming, "Hear, hear, hear! His Imperial Majesty, our most gracious master, hereby forbids any preacher, whoever he may be, from preaching here in Augsburg, excepting those whom his Majesty may appoint, upon pain of his Imperial Majesty's punishment and displeasure."

In itself, this measure was, of course, disadvantageous to the Protestants; and yet, on the other hand, it was favorable to them, in so far that it silenced the most violent of their theological opponents. Among them were, besides the celebrated professor of theology in Ingolstadt, Dr. John Eck; John Faber, court-preacher of King Ferdinand; John Cochlæus of Dresden, court-preacher of Duke George of Saxony; Dr. Conrad Wimpina, Rupert Elgersma, Wolfgang Rebdörfer and John Mensing,—all theologians from the University of Frankfort-on-the-Oder, and brought to Augsburg by the elector Joachim I. of Brandenburg. The preachers appointed by the emperor were of such a character as the elector represented in a letter to Luther of June 25 : "We are told that the preachers selected by the emperor in general do nothing more than read the text of the gospel, and that what they teach is childish and irrelevant stuff. Thus our God must keep silent at this Diet. We must not, however, attribute all the blame to our pious emperor, but rather to our enemies and the clergy who are strenuously opposed to us."

John Brentz reports to Isenman in Hall, on June 19, thus, in a postscript to his letter: "After I had written the above I hurried to the church to hear what the new preacher would have to say. I stood listening attentively; but, besides the text, I heard nothing but the general prayer for the living and the dead, and the whole service was concluded with a recitation of the Creed. There you have a preacher who is neither evangelical nor papal, but only a mere text-reader. Everybody laughs at this performance, and, really, it is a very laughable affair when you see it with your own eyes." But, to depict the entire mode of these services, Brentz adds: "After this service which they call preaching, they proceed to perform the mass, at which King Ferdinand with several princes is present; for the emperor usually sleeps till nine or ten o'clock, and holds his mass long after the others. On this occasion there is singing, organ-playing, attended by a crowd of people. You see French, Spanish, negroes—even negro women —Italians, Turks; and thus we here live in the midst of people of all nations. God grant that we were far removed from this character of people!"

This was the state of things in Augsburg until June 19, and during all this time our Luther in Coburg. He still suffered from attacks, as he calls them—"not ringing," but "thundering"—in his head. But, notwithstanding, he labored hard, for on June 19 he was able to inform Cordatus in Zwickau that he had finished the translation of Jeremiah, and that within two days he would have the *Confitemini* ready.

But from Augsburg he had learned only by common report that the emperor had arrived; he knew nothing more definite about it. Full three weeks* had elapsed, and he had received no letter from Augsburg. So great was his displeasure that he would not even believe Melanchthon when he told him that letters had been sent several times a week, but that they must have been lost. He in his impatience even declared that he would not read any letters which might subsequently come; and when Melanchthon was informed of this by Veit Dietrich, he sent letters unsealed to Veit and requested him to read them to Luther, whether he would hear them or not. No wonder that he expresses his indignation upon the silence of his Augsburg friends to some others.

While giving full vent to his displeasure,

---

* Stang, in his *Martin Luther*, erroneously says "three full months."

yet these letters contain many pious wishes for the emperor, "that pious noble blood Carolus" who is "a sheep among wolves," and whom his pretended friends have brought "into trouble and sorrow." They are also full of earnest entreaties in behalf of the elector and inquiries concerning him and other persons and the Diet.

He also reports progress in the work of translation and describes his own physical condition. He writes to two brothers studying in Wittenberg—Peter and Jerome Weller —who occupied his own house, and who had undertaken the training of his little son John, now four years of age. It was at this time that he wrote that letter to this boy which has been so often printed, and which is regarded as a model of a father's epistle to a child.*

In the mean time, the friends at Augsburg had written to him. Besides conveying the information of the arrival of the emperor and of the firmness of the elector, they also ex-

---

* See *Luther's Journeys*, p. 293.

press the deepest solicitude in his well-being and apologies for their silence. He received these communications on June 19, the day on which he had written to his friends in Wittenberg and other places. In his reply to Jonas on Monday, June 20, he rejoices over the steadfastness of the elector, and of Jonas himself. He recognizes therein the result of his unceasing prayer. He complains that Melanchthon suffers himself to be annoyed by his own thoughts and fears, entirely forgetting that the cause is in the hands of Him who said, "No one shall pluck you out of my hands." But toward the end he says: "Christ lives, and we shall also live even when we shall have died; and even when we are dead, He will care for our families. If I should be called to go to Augsburg, I would doubtless go, Christ willing; but I am considering with myself if I should not follow my own will and go without being called." From this we observe how intensely he longed to hasten to Augsburg and to appear before the emperor and the assembled States as he did at Worms with his "Here I stand; I cannot do otherwise. God help me! Amen." He also wrote on the same day to Philip Schæpf, the court-preacher of the landgrave Philip, and expresses his high gratification of the arrival of the landgrave at the Diet.

Melanchthon reported to Luther on June 19 that the emperor himself was conciliatory to the highest degree. Duke Henry of Brunswick had assured him that the emperor always opposed or moderated severe measures proposed by the enemies of the gospel, that the archbishop of Mainz and the duke of Brunswick were to some degree concerned in their behalf, but, on the other hand, that the Bavarian dukes were decidedly inimical to them, and that the papal legate Campegi was the author of all the oppressive and persecuting measures.

These letters had not yet reached the persons to whom they were addressed when, on Monday, June 20, the Diet was opened in the council-house.

A religious solemnity preceded the opening. In the procession to the cathedral the elector John, as chancellor, carried the naked sword before the emperor; for a mass, as the theologians replied to the demand of the emperor, was another thing than the Corpus Christi festival: Naaman served the king of Assyria in a heathen temple. But the most remarkable event accompanying this solemnity was the discourse which the papal orator, Vincentius Pimpinelli, archbishop of Rossa, delivered before the singing of the offertory. The principal theme was the eradication of the " Lutheran heresy;" he attributed all the misfortunes of Germany to it. Hence, if the key of Peter is not sufficient to unlock the stony hearts of the German princes, the sword of Peter must be employed to break them. In this style he discoursed in Latin for nearly an hour.

After the conclusion of the mass, his Imperial Majesty, accompanied by all the electors and States of the empire, numbering forty-two princes, proceeded to the council-hall with great pomp. When they had arrived at the hall, all the electors and princes took the places assigned to them; for King Ferdinand, there had been arranged an elevated chair, hung with gilt tapestry, opposite the imperial throne. The Diet was then opened.

The Pfalzgrave Frederick delivered a brief opening discourse in the name of the emperor. After this the imperial secretary, Alexander Schweiss, introduced the propositions to be submitted to the Diet. Those relating to what was called "The Religious Question" required "that the numerous complaints which the civil or spiritual authorities made against each other respectively should be submitted by both parties to the emperor in the Latin and German languages, who, with the divine guidance, would seek to effect a satisfactory adjustment of all difficulties." The propositions were generally expressed in gentle terms. All allusion to the Protestants and to Luther was wisely omitted. The States thanked the emperor, through the elector Joachim, for his attendance, and requested permission to make copies of the programme. At one o'clock the emperor, amid the same pompous display, rode back to the episcopal palace.

On the same afternoon the elector John invited his evangelical fellow-believers to his residence, and earnestly admonished them to cling unwaveringly to the cause of God and the pure doctrine and to defend it boldly, and to allow no threats of the enemy to tempt them to a denial of it.

On Wednesday, June 22, it was determined, on the part of the evangelicals, not to consent to any action on the subject of the Turkish troubles until the religious question had been settled. Even the Catholics favored this course of the proceedings. The result was that the Protestants received a command to have their Articles of Faith ready on Friday afternoon, June 24, at three o'clock. They asked for the postponement of a single day, but it was denied.

Accordingly, the evangelical princes, the deputies of the imperial cities of Nurnberg and Reutlingen, and a large number of learned men, among them twelve theologians, assembled in the residence of the elector for the purpose of taking final counsel upon the Confession. After every Article had been approved by every one present, it was resolved that the emperor should be requested to allow the Confession to be read in his presence before the assembled Diet. They then proceeded to signing it. Before they began, the Saxon theologians candidly declared to their sovereign that if he did not stand by them, they would themselves appear before the emperor. But with the words, "God forbid that you should exclude me! I will confess Christ with you," the elector John of Saxony took the pen and signed his name. Others followed him, such as the margrave George of Brandenberg, Duke John of Lüneburg, Landgrave Philip of Hesse, the electoral prince John Frederick of Saxony, Duke Francis of Lüneburg and Prince Wolfgang of Anhalt. The latter, on being advised to consider well what he was doing, seized the pen, and, with the remarkable words of heroism and faith, "I have engaged in many a stirring adventure for the gratification of others: why should I not, then, when it is necessary, in honor of and in obedience to my Lord and Saviour Jesus Christ, saddle my horse and by the sacrifice of my life hasten to receive the crown of glory in the world to come?" After these words he subscribed. The deputies from Nurnberg and Reutlingen followed his example.

But the most important step of all was to be taken, and that was the delivery of the Confession. It was to be done at the first session of the Diet, which commenced on Friday, June 24, at three o'clock in the afternoon. But, before all, the papal legate Campegi gave in his credentials and delivered a Latin speech similar in length and spirit to that of Pimpinelli. He also attributed all the existing troubles to the corrupting novelties introduced by the so-called Reformers, and intimated that the best method of suppressing them would be a return to the obedience of the emperor and the pope. The elector of Mainz in his reply lauded this discourse for its Christian character, its godly spirit and its tendency to the restoration of order in the German empire. After this the signers of the Confession demanded the hearing that was promised them. But delegates from the Austrian dominions had appeared, to lay before the Diet the troubles occasioned by the Turks. By order of the empéror they were admitted. Their oral complaints and a long written account of grievances occupied considerable time. Under these circumstances, the emperor postponed the hearing of the evangelical Confession, and requested that it be delivered to him. But the elector and the other princes were more concerned about its being read. If it were delivered without being publicly read, the Confession would most probably never have been heard of again; hence the Protestants insisted upon a hearing the following day. After a long consultation with King Ferdinand and the other Catholic powers, the emperor consented to hear it read the next day in his residence. This was extremely adverse to the wishes of the Protestants, for the largest apartment in the episcopal palace would not accommodate more than two hundred persons. Yet they adapted themselves to the circumstances, and gratefully accepted the imperial permission.

And thus, on June 25, 1530, on the day after the festival of St. John, the heroic forerunner of our Lord, in the afternoon, at four o'clock, the Augsburg Confession was read before the emperor and numerous German civil and ecclesiastical dignitaries in the chapel of the episcopal palace. The emperor commanded that the Latin copy should be read. But the elector John reminded the emperor that they were assembled on German soil, and upon this he granted permission to have it read in German. Two hours were occupied in the reading; but Dr. Christian Baier, the younger of the two chancellors, read to the end in a voice so loud that the multitude of people in the courtyard could hear every word. When the reading was finished, the chancellor, Dr. Brück, delivered both original copies to the emperor. It is said that Brück used the following language: "Most Gracious Emperor, this is such a Confession against which, with God's help, the gates of hell cannot prevail." The emperor took the copies; the German one he gave to the elector of Mainz, as the imperial archchancellor, to be deposited in the imperial archives, and retained the Latin copy for himself, to be taken to Brussels for custody in the state archives.

Neither of these original copies is extant. Duke Alba took away the Latin from Brussels, and the fate of the German is unknown. But the *result* remains. Guided by Melanchthon's hand and Luther's spirit, the evangelical powers and their theologians had carefully cherished the fruit of a purified faith and a reformed worship. The birth-hour of the evangelical Church had now struck. A Confession *in common* is essential to the character of the Church: up to this time the Protestants had no such common basis; from this time forth faith in the grace of God through Christ, or justification, which ensues from faith in the redemption "wrought by Christ," was the *special* bond of all Christians, and the word of God, as the only rule of all Christian faith and practice, was the *universal* bond of all those who protested against the meritoriousness of good works and the validity of human ordinances in the Church. In this there was no difference of opinion between John of Saxony and Philip of Hesse, or between Luther and Zwingli.

They were of one mind in the essentials of the Confession, but they divided upon the "is" and "signifies" in the Article of the Sacrament of the Body and Blood. Still, the landgrave Philip signed it. On the other hand, the cities of Strassburg, Constance, Lindau and Memmingen, who were inclined toward Zwingli's views, refused to subscribe it, and subsequently handed in a special Confession of Faith, which was drawn up by Martin Bucer, and which aimed at evading the controversy on the Lord's Supper by the use of ambiguous and indeterminate expressions. Afterward, on July 15, the cities of Heilbron, Kempten, Weinsheim and Weissenburg subscribed.

How the soul of Luther must have rejoiced when he received the letters from the elector and Melanchthon which informed him of the fact that the Confession was about to be publicly read on that day! How he must have shouted with rapture when he finally received the report: "The Confession has been read and delivered to the emperor"!

Jonas wrote to him more particularly toward the last of June, and informed him of the favorable impression which the Confession had made upon some who had been decided opponents of the Reformation. Among other things he says: "The archbishop of Salzburg is said in a private conversation to have expressed his wish that the sacrament should be administered in both kinds, that celibacy of the priesthood should be voluntary, and that the mass should be improved. He was also willing to allow liberty in relation to fasting and other church regulations. But that one monk should reform all was destructive of peace, and was not to be endured."

Bishop Stadion of Augsburg also set himself against the forcible measures of the Diet. He also reported that, notwithstanding all these favorable signs, Melanchthon was deeply dejected, and was inclined, for the sake of peace, to yield in many points, particularly in respect to the authority of the bishops. He begged Luther to write to Melanchthon on the subject, for he, Luther, "was the chariot of Israel and the leader thereof." Melanchthon at the same time wrote several letters to him and to Veit Dietrich, in which he spoke of the delivery of the Confession and of the favorable feeling of the archbishop of Mainz, the bishop of Augsburg and the duke of Brunswick, as well as of the unrelenting enmity of the elector Joachim and of Duke

George. He also complained of the melancholy condition in which he found himself and from which God alone could deliver him, and implored Luther's advice, wherein there might be some concession made to the opponents in the Articles of Both Kinds in the Sacraments, Sacerdotal Celibacy and the Mass. To Veit Dietrich he wrote expressly that amid the dangers by which they were surrounded in Augsburg, nothing was more indispensable than the counsel and consolation of Luther. The influence of Luther was everything to them; if he should forsake them, it could easily be imagined to what dreadful perils they would be exposed.

Luther, in his humility, had a quite different conception of his relation to the triumph of the gospel and of the exclusive help of God. Neither would he hear another word of yielding any farther, and it was not possible for his mighty spirit to sympathize with the timidity and despondency of his friend. On the day after he had received his letter he wrote (June 29): "I have received your Confession, and cannot comprehend how you want to know wherein we shall yield to our opponents. It is another thing with our elector. It is his duty to consider wherein he may yield if danger threatens him. As far as I am concerned, there has already been too much given up to them in the Confession; if they reject that, I do not see wherein I could yield any more, unless I shall before see their grounds and clearer Scripture proof than I have as yet seen. The matter engages my attention day and night. I revolve it in my mind; I dispute with myself and bring up in array the whole Scriptures. The result is that I am more and more convinced of the truth of our doctrine, and I am therein strengthened every day, that I, with God's help, will not consent that anything more shall be taken away from it, let the consequences be what they may." After he had mentioned that their prayers for him had helped to break the power of the evil spirit who had buffeted him, and that he now was in good health, he proceeds to impart consolation to Melanchthon in a style eminently characteristic.

In a postscript he adds that he did not

more particularly reply to the question concerning the points to be surrendered, because Melanchthon did not specify what the opponents demanded, and thus concludes: "I am ready to surrender everything except the gospel; that they must not take from us. I will not consent to anything that is contrary to the gospel."

He wrote letters of encouragement and comfort to other friends.

His book on *The Recall from Purgatory* was begun about this time.

No more striking exhibition of Luther's confidence in God, of his delight in prayer, and generally of his evangelical spiritual-mindedness can be made than that which we observe in Veit Dietrich's letter to Melanchthon of June 30. "I cannot," says he, "sufficiently admire his firmness, composure, faith and hope in these trying times. But he braces himself up against them by a diligent use of the word of God. No day goes by in which he does not spend at least three hours in prayer.

"I was once fortunate enough to hear him

pray. What an ardor, what a faith, in his words! He prayed so devoutly as one should speak with God; with such hope and confidence as one who speaks with his father. 'I know,' said he, 'that Thou art our dear God and Father; hence I am certain that Thou wilt destroy the persecutors of Thy children. If Thou doest it not, the danger is Thine as well as ours, for the whole cause is Thine; what we have done, that we were compelled to do; and hence, dear Father, Thou must protect us.'"

Veit continues: "When I heard him utter these words in prayer with a clear voice, my heart leaped in me for joy, because he so strenuously pleaded the promises as if he were certain that everything must occur just as he desired it. Hence I do not doubt that his prayer will be of unspeakable service in this lost cause (as some apprehend) which is to be considered in the Diet."

Concerning the impression which the death of Luther's father made upon him, and of the manner in which he consoled himself by the use of the Scriptures, Veit had previously written to Luther's wife. "I beg you," says he, "that you will not be uneasy about the doctor. He is, thank God! well and in good spirits, and has now recovered from the blow which his father's death gave him, although at first it was very severe. As soon as he saw Hans Reynick's letter he said to me, 'My father is dead.' He immediately took up his psalter, went into his chamber, and there grieved so excessively that he was quite unwell all next day. After that was over, he recovered his usual composure."

Katharine sent the likeness of one of her children in her letter of condolence, which gratified him beyond expression.

CHAPTER V.

FROM THE FIRST PROCEEDINGS OF THE OPPONENTS TO THE TIME OF THE READING OF THE CATHOLIC "CONFUTATION."

(FROM JUNE 1 TO AUG. 3, 1530.)

LUTHER had now been nearly three months in the fortress of Coburg, and was compelled to remain three months longer.

The detention had become almost intolerably wearisome. He ardently desired, as early as the middle of July, that the elector and his friends might be released from the duty of remaining at Augsburg, and that he himself might be permitted to leave Coburg. When the Diet had reached its culmination by the reading and delivery of the Confession, he saw that nothing more was to be expected, but the Diet " dragged its slow length along " until November 19. From June 26 to August 3 the " Confutation of the Augsburg Confession" was considered; then, as this Confutation did not accomplish its design, the restoration of harmony with the Protestants was discussed from August 3 to September 7; and finally, as this also failed, the subject of employing force to bring back everything as it was before 1517 was debated from September 7 to November 19.

When, on the day after the delivery of the Confession—Sunday, June 26—the emperor consulted with the Catholic States as to the course now to be pursued, there were not wanting those who advised an immediate renewal of the edict of Worms and forcible suppression of the innovations. Others, and among them King Ferdinand, thought it better to refer the Confession to a committee of learned and impartial men for examination. Others advised the preparation of a treatise which would refute the Confession. This last suggestion was approved by the emperor; and Dr. John Eck, with nineteen other theologians—all decided enemies of the Confession—was appointed to write what was called a "Confutation." By this partial act the original intention of the emperor "to hear every man's opinion of both parties," and thus, if possible, to secure a peaceful means of reconciliation, was practically nullified and the coming result expressed.

The Catholic theologians had finished their task by the 13th of July. It was, however, no refutation, but a long series of calumnies against their opponents, and hence, in the judgment of the emperor, was not fit to be brought before the assembly. So decided was the displeasure of the emperor with this paper that, as Spalatin says, "he rumpled and rolled it so violently that of two hundred and eighty leaves only twelve remained whole." In consequence of a new order of the emperor, the learned Dominican Faber, the court-preacher of Ferdinand, undertook another refutation; and thus the time passed until Wednesday, August 3, when this Confutation was read in the same episcopal chapel in which the evangelical Confession had achieved its brilliant triumph on the 25th of June previously. This intermediate time the emperor employed in forcing, if possible, the elector of Saxony to an apostasy from the gospel by threatening the refusal of the investiture so long as he persisted in his disloyalty to the Romish Church. Charles also employed various measures of questionable honesty in attempting to create dissension between the deputies from the imperial cities and the princes. But both attempts failed. The elector as well as the other subscribers to the Confession continued faithful to the gospel, and the delegates from the cities maintained their previous relations to the princes.

Melanchthon was well aware of the painful anxiety with which Luther in Coburg longed for intelligence from Augsburg. The former also in his timidity felt the need of Luther's counsel, and in his dejection the need of his comfort. In a series of letters to Veit Deitrich and to Luther, he communicated to him the most important events. Besides that which we have just reported concerning the Confutation and the steadfastness of the Protestant States, Luther heard, through Melancthon, that among the opponents of the Confession the papal legate Campegi and

Duke George of Saxony were the most violent. On the other hand, several of the Catholic States were favorably disposed. The archbishop of Mainz had strenuously recommended peaceable measures, but he did not succeed, and on this account absented himself from the Diet on the next day. The bishop of Augsburg was of the same mind. Especially was the *sister of the emperor, the widowed queen Maria of Hungary*, to be commended. She was a woman of heroic spirit, at the same time of distinguished piety and practical wisdom, and tried to win the favor of her brother in behalf of the Protestants; of course she was obliged to use great tact and discretion in the pursuit of her design. Melanchthon also stated that the cautious friend of the Reformation, Erasmus, in a letter to the emperor, had heartily approved of those Articles which were particularly discussed—the Sacrament in Both Kinds, Priestly Marriages and the Abolition of the Private Masses; on the other hand, that Œcolampadius had written against Luther; that Zwingli had sent in a printed Confession of Faith which proved that he was not of sound mind, for he persevered in his old errors on original sin and the Lord's Supper; and that Capito and Bucer arrived at the same time from Strassburg.

Besides this, Melanchthon sent a list of calumnious writings of Catholic theologians against Luther, as well as Melanchthon's expositions of certain theological principles, and begged Luther's judgment upon them. When Faber's "Confutation" was read, on August 3, Melanchthon wrote thus to Luther on August 6: "Finally, we have heard the reading of the Confutation and the emperor's decision. The latter is hard enough. For before the Confutation was read the emperor declared that he would abide by the opinions therein expressed and required the princes to do the same; if not, then he, as protector of the Church, would allow of no division in Germany. This was the substance of his discourse. Threatening as it was, after the reading of the Confutation we felicitated each other heartily, for it is a childish production throughout. It is the most miserable of all the miserable books ever written by Faber."

This was the reason why, as Melanchthon

further reports, when the princes requested a copy of it, the emperor promised them one on the next day only upon the express condition that it should not be published nor copied. All this and his other communications, if not without confiding prayer for divine help, are yet accompanied to a still greater extent with expressions of discouragement and dejection.

During the progress of these events and reports from Augsburg, Luther continued to be as active in his writings, prayers and correspondence amid much physical suffering as he had been in the preceding three months of his sojourn in the fortress.

Of his writings at this time, we must make particular mention of his *Exposition of Ps. cxviii*. He could send copies to the abbot Frederick in Nurnberg, to whom he dedicated it, and to the poet Coben Hesse, then living in Nurnberg, only on August 22, because the printers at Wittenberg had been particularly tardy. He ardently expresses his admiration of this psalm, and designates it as "the beautiful Confitemini."

He had scarcely finished this when he commenced the *Sermon upon the Duty of Parents to Send their Children to School.* This is one of the most capital treatises of those times on the general subject of school-training and on the necessity of universal education. It shows clearly how far in advance of his times Luther was on that subject, which Protestantism has ever regarded as essential to the extension and perpetuation of the cause.

About this time he also wrote *Thoughts on the Abolition of Monasticism and of the Mass by the Princes.* Cœlestin reports that both queens—Anna, the wife of Ferdinand, and Maria, the widowed queen of Hungary—had asked questions of Luther relative to these subjects.

The Recall from Purgatory is dated July, 1530, and *Lies concerning the Keys* was written while the former was going through the press. At the same time he expounded the one hundred and seventeenth psalm and dedicated it to his patron of Coburg, the knight Hans von Sternberg, from which dedication we learn that Sternberg had made a pilgrimage to Jerusalem, and that Luther had listened to the narrative of his tour "with supreme delight."

His severe and protracted labor upon the Prophets occasioned such violent attacks of headache and exhaustion that he abandoned the work temporarily in August. Only Hosea had been finished during some intervals of comparative exemption from sickness.

During the month of July he wrote a large number of letters to some of the highest ecclesiastical dignitaries, to the elector and to his friends, and yet, amid all these perplexing labors, he sometimes complains of want of employment!

Everything connected with the Confession, and all the subjects which at that time engaged the attention of the Reformers, were treated in these letters. He cheered them on in their perilous enterprise and animated the desponding. He implored them to make no further concessions, but to stand by the truth unflinchingly. He thanks them for their sympathy, but declares that their extreme anxiety about his health and their fears that he overexerted his strength were groundless.

CHAPTER VI.

FROM THE READING OF THE CATHOLIC CONFUTATION TO LUTHER'S DEPARTURE FROM COBURG.

(FROM AUG. 3 TO OCT. 6, 1530.)

IMMEDIATELY after the reading of the Confutation important events occurred in Augsburg.

As early as Friday, August 5, the emperor ordered the evangelical princes and States to reunite with the Catholic States on the basis of the Confutation, and, in the event of their refusal, they might expect coercive measures to be pursued. Unawed by this threat, the Protestants, certain that their Confession was founded on God's word, and, firmly resolved not to depart from that word, would not comply with this requirement. The result was that the Catholic party proposed to treat with the Protestants once more by a commission. The emperor approved of this proposition, and a commission of sixteen Catholic princes, bishops and deputies met together on Saturday, August 6.

Another important event occurred on the same day: it was the sudden withdrawal of the landgrave Philip of Hesse. Against the express will of the emperor, whose permission he had requested, but had not obtained, and without the knowledge of his fellow-believers, he left Augsburg on August 6 and travelled toward home. His councillors remained in Augsburg. He left behind him a letter to the elector of Saxony, entreating him not to depart from the word of God in the least degree, and declared that "he was ready to sacrifice life, property, country and subjects for it." As the ground of his departure, he gave the serious sickness of his wife. The presumption was that in the present circumstances he would take no further part in the Diet, and held it to be more advisable to prepare himself for an armed defence of the gospel. A new turn was given to the condition of things by this unexpected event. The emperor could not but discern that the measure of his demands was full. The displeasure at the imperial requirement that the Protestants should submit God's word and their conscience to an external power had reached its limits, and outward obedience to the emperor was only maintained by their continuance in Augsburg. They still hoped that the emperor, agreeably to his declaration in the Diet that he "would graciously hear the opinions of both sides," would restore peace and unity. By the departure of the landgrave this limit was transcended.

There was one thing yet which might have secured the desired peace. At the meeting of the commission on August 6 the bishop of Augsburg proposed that some important privileges should be granted to the Protestants, or, in other words, that some concessions should be made to them. This measure was not approved, and no progress toward reconciliation was made. A new measure was now adopted, and a committee from both parties was appointed to deliberate upon a method of securing unity on individual doctrines and usages. At the beginning, from August 16 to August 20, there were fourteen—two princes, two lawyers, and three theologians from each side. Melanchthon was the Protestant speaker, and Eck the Catholic. From the 24th of August the number was reduced to seven, and really it now seemed as if an agreement would take place, as so many concessions were made on both sides.

But it did not reach this issue. On the other hand, things took a quite different turn, which we can learn in the fewest words from a letter which Luther wrote to Hausman in Zwickau on September 23: "You have probably already heard that certain judges, and among them Melanchthon, were chosen to consult about securing unity in doctrine and faith. But, as they could not agree, they again referred the matter to the emperor, and they are now waiting for his decision, although it would appear from recent letters that they have brought up other means of reconciliation, which have not been communicated to me. At the first meeting our opponents required that we should yield the private masses, and also to retain both canons with the comments, and to understand the word *sacrifice* in the sense of a commemorative mediatory offering; also that we should agree that it be left to the liberty of every one to partake of the Lord's Supper in one or in both kinds; finally, that we should consent that the monks and clergy who were married should be divorced without delay and return again to the cloisters, and that they should no longer be regarded as having been married. If we agreed to this, they would consent to the sacrament in both kinds, and to bear with these divorced wives on account of the children until a future council, just as it is granted to others to live in unmarried communities. Here you see, my dear Nicolas, the insolent pride of Satan, who as a strong man leads at his will those whom he has captured, and is not ashamed to inflate them with such abominable, disgraceful and dishonoring propositions. But our men would not yield to them, but consented to reinstate the bishops in their jurisdiction upon condition that they would diligently make provision for and encourage the preaching of the gospel and abolish all abuses, and also some holy days. But nothing was accomplished. Our adversaries are boldly bent upon destruction; an irresistible destiny drives them on."

This was the condition of things in the beginning of December between the Catholic majority, headed by the emperor, and the Protestant minority, led by the elector John. But Luther himself contributed very much to the firmness with which the elector John, his chancellor Brück and Melanchthon—too much inclined to concession—maintained the rights of the gospel. Specially beautiful and elevating is the letter which Luther wrote to Brück already before the reading of the Catholic Confutation, wherein he seeks to animate him with confidence in the help of God. It is dated August 5. We shall content ourselves with some extracts from it:

"I have written several times to my gracious ruler, and to others of our party, that I begin to think I have overdone it, especially in writing to him as though I doubted that God's comfort and help were enjoyed by him in a greater degree than by me. But I did it at the suggestion of several of our friends, some of whom are so dejected and anxious as though God had forgotten us. But He cannot forget us: He must first forget Himself. In that case our cause would not be His cause, and our doctrine would not be His word. But if we are certain of it, and do not doubt that it is His cause and word, then most surely is our prayer heard and the help we need is already ·prepared for us. That cannot fail. For He says, 'Can a woman forget her sucking child, that she should not have compassion on the son of her womb? Yea, she may forget, yet will I not forget thee!'

"I have recently witnessed two miracles. The first was when I was looking out of the window. I beheld the stars in the heavens and the whole beautiful vault of God, and yet I nowhere saw pillars on which the Builder had set this vault; and yet the heavens did not fall down and the vault still stands unmoved. Now, there are some who are looking for pillars; and, as they cannot see them, they are trembling with fear that the heavens will certainly fall, and for no other reason than that they cannot see the columns. If they could see them, then the heavens would stand and all would be plain enough.

"The other was that I saw heavy, dark clouds floating over us in such immense masses that they might be compared to a mighty ocean; and yet I saw no foundation on which they could rest, nor any vessel in which they could be caught; and still they did not fall upon us, but saluted us with an angry look and dispersed. When they had departed, the rainbow beautifully illuminated the base on which the clouds rested and the vault above us. The base and vault were so fragile that they also melted away in the clouds and seemed to be rather a lustrous foam, as if shining through colored glass, than such an immense base, so as to lead one to be as apprehensive of it as of the enormous weight of water. And yet the fact was that it was the apparently infirm floating vapor that sustained the water and protected us. Yet there are some who pay more attention to, and have more fear of, the water and the thick clouds and heavy weight than the light and thin vapor, for they are anxious to know the sustaining force of such floating masses; and because they cannot do that, they fear that the clouds will occasion an everlasting deluge."

He proceeds to stimulate his friends to

steadfastness, and hopes to hear of the eventual triumph of the gospel cause.

After the reading of the Confutation, the character of which was communicated to him, he wrote to Melanchthon thanking God that the document was so utterly indefensible, and encouraged him with the exclamation, "But now strike heavy blows with all your might!" When the elector had sent him the resolutions of both parties concerning the sacrament, private masses, the right of princes to reform their own subjects, the canon of the mass and church ordinances, and requested his opinion concerning them, he sent elaborate answers on each distinct point, displaying extraordinary acuteness and scriptural knowledge.

The persevering determination of Luther to stand immovably upon the ground of God's word and the disinclination of the opponents to submit to this condition—or, as it is briefly expressed in Luther's letter to Spalatin on August 26, "because the pope did not want a reconciliation" and Luther would not consent to anything not consistent with the Scriptures—necessarily broke up the meeting of the small committee on August 31, and the whole affair was submitted to the decision of the emperor. From this time forth there was nothing more to expect from the Diet. The Protestants had to be satisfied with the fact that they had borne their testimony to the faith and to have aimed at securing peace. They had come to hear whether the opponents would sanction their doctrines or not, and had left it to them to do as they pleased.

The decision of the emperor could be anticipated, and it was not long in coming. As early as September 7 the rumblings of the coming storm were heard. The emperor had it proclaimed to the Protestants that he was ready to submit the subject to a general council. The appeal to a general council was adopted, and the emperor threatened that, in case of disobedience, he would exercise his authority "as guardian and protector of the Church." Notwithstanding, the Protestants replied "that they had never swerved from the word of God nor adopted a new rule of faith; that they were ready at any moment to accept everything which could be substantiated by the Holy Scriptures; that they could not grant more, and on this ground it was impossible for them to enter into any further negotiations."

Thus was accomplished on the Protestant side what Luther had long wished for, and what he thought was best in a correct estimate of the condition of things. But the emperor himself broke up all further fellowship with them on September 22. On the evening of that day he summoned the evangelical princes and deputies from the cities to the episcopal palace, and communicated to them the proposal adopted by the Catholic States to dissolve the Diet. With regard to the subject of religion, "the elector of Saxony and the five princes and the six cities" should hold with the Church all the Articles not finally settled until a general council, to be held on April of the next year, not in any manner to aggrieve the adherents of the ancient faith, to abstain from all innovations and to press no one to join "their sect," as they had done heretofore. It was in vain that the elector of Saxony, for himself and his associates, protested against this resolution. Neither was it of any avail that Melanchthon handed in through Chancellor Brück his so-called *Apology of the Augsburg Confession*, which he had then already sketched out. The emperor and the pope had spoken.

Under such circumstances, nothing else seemed to be left to the elector than to abandon the Diet. Four weeks before, the deputies from Nurnberg had written home: "The elector of Saxony has despatched his baggage on four wagons. You may expect that before long, there will be nobody remaining here." On September 14 the electoral prince on his return home met Luther in Coburg. The elector John took leave of the emperor. When he appeared before him in the Diet to announce his departure, it is said that he made the declaration which according to others was made in the same words by Chancellor Brück when he delivered the Confession: "I am most thoroughly convinced that my doctrine, as it is declared in the Confession, is founded upon the Holy Scriptures, and that the gates of hell shall not prevail against it." Perhaps he only repeated Brück's utterance. It is certain, however, that the emperor extended his hand with the words, " Uncle, I did not expect that from your Grace." The elector left the assembly with tears which were the evidence of deceived hopes and profound grief. This occurred on Friday, September 23, after a sojourn of twenty-one weeks in Augsburg. He left his councillors behind. On the same day, John the Constant pursued his journey with his retinue toward Nurnberg, on his return to Torgau by way of Coburg.

In the mean time, Luther had done many things and had diverse experience in Coburg.

In reference to the Diet, besides the transactions with the opponents, two important considerations touching the Protestant communion claimed his most earnest attention.

The first was the relation to the Confession of Zwingli and of his associates and adherents, Bucer, Hedio and Capito. It has already been stated that, in the beginning of July, Melanchthon had informed Luther that Zwingli had sent in a Confession of Faith whose doctrines of the Lord's Supper and of original sin had received Melanchthon's highest disapprobation. From the same source Luther had heard that Bucer and Capito, who, with Hedio, represented the cities of Strassburg, Memmingen, Constance and Lindau, which were rather inclined toward Zwingli's doctrine, had shortly before July 14 arrived at Augsburg; that Bucer, the preacher at Strassburg, seemed—in words, at least—to be inclined toward Luther's doctrine; and that on this account negotiations were opened between the Lutherans and Bucer. Bucer and Capito also treated with Luther on this subject by letter, but nothing was accomplished. For this reason, Bucer, with the knowledge of the elector of Saxony, was sent, toward the end of September, to Coburg to treat with Luther personally. But the result was not satisfactory. Luther had declared that he was ready to cherish the kindest brotherly affection and to promote unity, but that the Zwinglians must cling to God's word alone and give up their subtle and unsubstantial explanations. Bucer parted from Luther "with the kindest feelings," but could not bring about a real unity. In consequence of this, the Confession of the Four Cities—usually called the Tetrapolitana—prepared by Bucer, was delivered to the emperor, but which did not receive any consideration as a theological memorial. The same fate awaited the Confession of Zwingli.

The other event which touched Luther's heart more tenderly, and which seemed like opposition in the camp, was the fierce displeasure which the Nurnberg deputies and the Hessian theologians manifested toward Melanchthon for his disposition to yield to the enemy. His inclination to allow the bishops to exercise certain high civil prerogatives, especially excited the indignation of the Nurnberg deputies and brought down upon him the severest reproaches. They attributed his conduct in this affair to the fear of displeasing the parties in power—in other words, to an abject fear of man. One of them, the otherwise worthy Jerome Baumgartner, the same who five years before had so perseveringly sought the hand of Katharine de Bora, wrote on September 15 to Spengler in Nurnberg: "Hence I beg you, for God and His word's sake, that you will also contribute to this end, and write to Dr. Martin Luther that he through whom God has again given His word to the world would powerfully oppose Philip and request the pious princes, especially his own sovereign, to warn him and exhort him to steadfastness. For at this Diet there is no man who has done more harm to the gospel than Philip." But he adds: "I do not write this willingly of him, because until this time he was highly esteemed;" and he concluded with the important declaration: "But now the day of trial has come, and, for my part, by God's help, neither Luther nor Philip shall be so greatly honored by me that I would follow either of them contrary to God's word."

Not only did Spengler write on this subject to Luther, but he was so beset on all sides with complaints about Melanchthon and his friends, Jonas, Brentz, etc., that on September 20 he wrote to Melanchthon and Jonas and begged to hear the particulars, and whether it was true that they, in the concessions made to the enemy, had claimed his acquiescence; and in the letter to Jonas he exclaims: "If this is so, then the devil has brought about a charming disagreement among ourselves."

On the other hand, Melanchthon had already written to Luther on Monday, August 29: "I am severely censured by our friends that I have adjudged to the bishops their privileges. For the large majority, once accustomed to liberty, and free from episcopal authority, will not allow the former burdens to be imposed upon them again, and the States of the empire hate episcopal rule."

Melanchthon's other letters, even to the time of his departure from Augsburg with the elector, are full of similar complaints and melancholy apprehensions for the future in regard to the government of the Church.

To Luther himself, shortly before, he sent the last packet of papers by Camerarius in Nurnberg. But Luther, animated by an intense anxiety to maintain peace and harmony among the believers and by a strong personal attachment to Melanchthon, took him, as it were, under his protection, and especially sought to pacify the friends in Nurnberg.

He also wrote to Lazarus Spengler on the same subject on September 28, and condoled with him upon his regret of having offended Melanchthon.

We must yet consider the labors of Luther during the latter period of his sojourn at Coburg. We mention first his *Letter on Translation*. He sent it on September 12 to the printer Link at Nurnberg. We cannot read this production without highly appreciating him as a translator of the Bible and regarding his translation with holy reverence. For a proper comprehension of it, however, we must remember that his well-known enemy, Jerome Emser, in Dresden, secretary and councillor of Duke George of Saxony, after the prohibition of the translation of the New Testament in the duchy of Saxony (1522), was ordered by Duke George to prepare a translation. He freely used Luther's, or corrupted it, and yet in his preface he heaps shameless abuses upon Luther personally and upon his translation.

Although Emser died in 1527, yet his very imperfect New Testament, with its preface and its calumnies, continued to live. Hence Luther wrote his *Letter on Translation* as a defence of himself and for instruction to his contemporaries, and, among other things, he says: "I have bestowed most diligent care upon translating, that I might give the original in pure, clear German, and it often happened to us that we sometimes spent fourteen days—even three or four weeks—in trying to get the meaning of a single word, and even then we sometimes failed. In working at Job, for instance, Philip, Aurogallus and I could sometimes scarcely finish three lines in four days. Now, as it is translated and printed, anybody can read it and master it; he can run over three or four pages with his eyes and not stumble once, but he is not aware what stones and logs were lying there over which he can now pass as smoothly as over a planed board, but which we removed out of the way only at the expense of toil and sweat. It is easy to plough where the field is all clean and smooth, but to remove the stumps and prepare the field nobody wants or likes to do. We must not ask the letters of the Hebrew, Greek or Latin languages how to speak German, but we must ask the mother in the family, the children in the street, the common man in the market-place, and we must particularly observe how they speak, and translate accordingly; then they understand and notice that we are speaking German to them." He continues: "I can declare with a good conscience that I have faithfully and diligently pursued this work, and have been actuated by no unworthy motive, for I have never asked or received a single farthing for it; neither have I sought my own honor therein. God knows that I have done it only to serve dear Christians and to the glory of One who is seated on high, who is constantly bestowing so many favors upon me that if I had worked at my translation a thousand times harder, I would not have acquired merit enough to live only an hour or to have one sound eye. I owe all that I am and have to His grace and mercy —yea, to His precious blood and bitter agony; hence everything I do shall be done for His glory with all my heart. Let the bungler (Emser) malign me; pious Christians will praise me together with their Lord Jesus, and I am already richly rewarded when a single Christian recognizes me as a faithful workman."

Besides these more serious labors, he sometimes amused himself in writing some literary trifles, which have been preserved to us in the form of fables, which are a good imitation of the ancient Æsop. Mathesius, his contemporary and biographer, dwells at length upon these productions of his hours of recreation, and praises them for their practical wisdom and fidelity to nature.

During the time that Luther was corresponding with friends in Nurnberg and Augsburg concerning Melanchthon, he informed the latter, on September 15, that the day before the electoral prince, with Count Albert of Mansfeld, had unexpectedly arrived at Coburg Castle, and had presented him with a gold ring. Concerning this he writes: "That I should know that I was not born to wear gold, the ring immediately fell from my finger on the floor (for it was too large for me). Upon this I said, 'Thou art a worm, and no man; such presents should be made to Faber and Eck; a leaden bullet is better suited to thee, or a rope round thy neck.'" These words were not merely jocular, but one of the numerous evidences of his humility and modesty, which his letters from Coburg sufficiently show. To give only two examples. On August 24 he wrote thus to Melanchthon: "Recently I have been attacked with a soreness of the throat. If Christ only conquers, it will be nothing that Luther is overcome; for he will conquer when Christ achieves the vicrory." Two days after he wrote to Brenz upon his exposition of the prophet Amos, and sets forth the superior character of Brenz's style in comparison with his own with a candor, modesty and self-consciousness of which great minds alone are capable.

That ring which Luther received on September 14, 1530, from the hands of the Ernestine electoral prince John Frederick, was presented more than one hundred years after (1652) to the Albertine electoral prince John George I. by Luther's great-grandson, John Melchior Luther, a councillor in Wurzen. The prince, who died in October, 1656, took it with him into his coffin, and the cathedral at Freiberg has for over two hundred years enclosed this memorial of Luther's residence at Coburg.

During all this time the Diet at Augsburg had entirely lost all attraction for Luther. The ravens, also, on the south side of the fortress, had long dissolved their Diet, and storm and rain raged so fearfully around it that Luther, suffering from bronchitis and toothache, became heartily weary of his stay. And yet he did not avail himself of the privilege of travelling home with him, granted by the prince during his visit on September 14. "I begged him," he writes to Melanchthon, "to permit me to await you here on your return home, that I might wipe away your sweat after this hot bath."

On September 23, just as he was about despatching to Hausman the letter mentioned above relating to the peace negotiations, he received from the elector himself the information that he would leave Augsburg on that day. On the next day he sent the elector's letter to his wife, and wrote: "I hope now, God willing, I will be at home with you in fourteen days."

He received some presents during his residence at Coburg, among which was one from Melanchthon, which was a picture of the siege of Vienna in 1529. Another from a titled friend in Augsburg gave occasion to the following letter: "The two boxes of sweetmeats kindly sent by you have been received, for which I return my sincere thanks. . . . During this summer I have suffered much from roaring in my head. I do not know the origin of it, for in all things I have been abstemious. I think it is the work of that angry fellow from hell who cannot endure me in his kingdom upon earth, but perhaps God will soon help me out of it, amen; with grace, amen. It gives me pain to hear that God's word in Augsburg must keep still and give place. It is not specially a good sign. God help me and us all! Amen."

He congratulated the elector on his departure from Augsburg in these words, written October 3: "I most heartily rejoice that your Electoral Grace has, with God's help, escaped out of the hell of Augsburg. I have commended the cause to my God. He has begun it—that I know; He will also carry it out—that I believe. As it is His and it is not left to our hands nor skill, I will see who those are that want to be so refined and expert as to boast that they can do more than God himself. Let things proceed as they are doing, in the name of God. Let them go on and threaten as they will, but to carry out and perfect their schemes, that they will not be allowed to do."

At the same time, as a faithful servant of his electoral master, he brings to his notice various oppressions which the officers of the household had exercised upon their subordinates, and which he himself had observed during his six months' "housekeeping here in Coburg." He also presented, in the name of the "keeper of the common treasury," a "petition," with the apology "that he could not decline doing this, because I am a guest here." He also begged the elector to excuse "Dr. Apel" for absenting himself from the castle.

Thus many of his letters written at Coburg contain petitions and recommendations in behalf of others who sought his good offices and his influence.

But nothing could give his residence at Coburg and his correspondence a more brilliant termination than his letter to the court-musician of Bavaria, Ludwig Senfel of Munich, dated October 4. To secure its safe delivery in Senfel's hands, he sent it to the Nurnberger deputy in Augsburg, Jerome Baumgartner, with a letter, at the conclusion of which he makes a sportive allusion to the former tender inclination of Baumgartner to Katharine. He says: "I salute you in the name of my lady-master, formerly your flame, and I will tell her this when I shall get home. I now sometimes tease her with mentioning your name."

The principal design of writing to Senfel, which was in Latin (for the chapelmaster was well acquainted with that language), was to request him to compose a piece for four voices on one of his favorite hymns, *In pace in id ipsum*. But the letter was chiefly made up of a eulogy on music, which entitles Luther's name to hold an eminent place in the history of sacred music especially. *This last letter from Coburg* is the following:

"Grace and peace in Christ! Although my name is so depised that I am apprehensive that this letter, my dear Ludwig, may not be kindly received or read by you, yet my love for music, with which God has so adorned and endowed you, has overcome my fears. This reverence for the divine art inspires me with the hope that this letter will be of no disadvantage to you. For who, even among the Turks, would blame him who loves the art and praises the artist? I also commend and honor your dukes of Bavaria, even if they are not very well disposed toward me, yet because they cherish music and hold it in high esteem. There is no doubt that the seeds of many virtues are lodged in those minds which are devoted to music, and those who are not moved by it I regard as stocks and stones. For we know that music is intolerable to the devils. I maintain the opinion, and am not ashamed to declare it, that, next to theology, there is no art that can be compared with music; because it alone, after theology, does that which otherwise theology alone accomplishes—namely, in tranquillizing the mind and promoting a cheerful, happy temper. The proof of this is that the devil, who occasions gloomy apprehensions and turbulent confusion, flies before music and its sweet sounds with almost the same celerity as from the language of theology. The prophets have employed no art except music; they did not clothe their theology in the language of art or of geometry or arithmetic or astronomy, but in music. Theology and music were closely associated, and hence they declared the truth in psalms and songs. But why should I even begin to commend it on so small a sheet of paper, and paint, or rather disfigure, a great subject on a narrow canvas? But my ardent inclination to it bubbles up in me so violently that I am often refreshed and rescued from deep despondency and discouragement.

"I appeal to you again, and pray that if you have any melody to the hymn, *In pace in id ipsum*, that you would copy it and send it to me. I have known that hymn from my youth and it has always quickened me, but I have never heard it sung by several voices together. But I will not ask you to take the trouble of composing a new tune for it, but I hope you may already have one. . . . I have already begun to sing this hymn in view of my early death, and am very anxious to hear it sung according to a suitable tune. If you have none and do not know one, I hereby send it to you; so that after my death, if you will please, you may compose a melody for it. The Lord Jesus be with you eternally. Amen! Excuse my boldness and loquacity. Salute your whole musical choir very reverently."

In the mean time, the elector had arrived in Nurnberg on September 27. To the question of the Nurnberger council, What is to be done under present circumstances? he answered, that he firmly hoped that God would graciously protect and uphold His word and its confessors; that he would himself enjoin it upon his spiritual and civil councillors to cherish and promote the cause to the utmost of their power; and that the council of Nurnberg, in fellowship with the other cities of the Augsburg Confession, would do the same. Time would determine what other further measures should be pursued.

A few days after, the elector, with Melanchthon, Jonas, Spalatin, Agricola and the other retinue, came to Coburg. What a meeting this was to Luther after six months' separation, and after such momentous events in view of a not less momentous future! However, the basis of a permanent communion was laid with the Augsburg Confession. Confidence in God and a consciousness of right steeled the hearts of these pious men for every conflict before them. Luther was then, and continued to be, the ruling spirit, when, two years after, on August 16, 1532, the elector John the Constant was called away from faith to sight, and John Frederick the Magnanimous, the last elector of the Ernestine branch, became the successor of his father, who died in the faith of the Augsburg Confession.

On the 5th or 6th of October, Luther left Coburg in company of the elector; on Saturday, the 8th, they reached Altenberg; the following day they arrived at Grimma; on the 10th, at Torgau, where Luther on the next Sunday, the 16th, preached in the electoral castle chapel.

The Diet still continued to November 19. On this day the dissolution was solemnly proclaimed. The time previously determined at which the Protestants should return to the Roman Church, April 15, 1531, was mentioned in the proclamation. The refractory were threatened with the application of force,

Thus ended the Diet of Augsburg in the year 1530.

On November 24 the emperor Charles, with King Ferdinand and many followers of exalted rank, hastened aw&y from Augsburg and proceeded to Cologne. Quiet was restored to the theatre of the Diet. The curtain had fallen.

Soon after his return from Coburg, Luther wrote two papers relating to the Diet. One was *Comments of Martin Luther on the Alleged Imperial Edict.* By that he meant the final decree of the Diet. He called it "Imperial Edict" as far as it was accepted by the emperor and his adherents, but by far not by the States of the empire. Besides, the seal of the council of Augsburg was not attached to it, and this was contrary to the standing and acknowledged order of things. He used the word "alleged" because he by no means regarded "the pious emperor Charles" as the originator or author, but the traitors and ungodly men who used the emperor as their instrument. These comments illustrated the demands and threats of the edict in the light of the gospel and of justice.

The other writing, or paper, was *Admonition to my dear Germans.* This is a Christian, patriotic warning against everything unchristian and *ungerman* in the Christian German Church. Alluding to the fruitlessness of his *Admonition to the Clergy*, he now turns to the German people, represents the danger which now threatens the gospel, and in opposition to his former opinions he now, for the first time, openly declares the necessity of opposing armed force to any armed attack that might be made upon the gospel. In the mean time, and before the appearance of these two writings, the meeting of the Protestant princes and cities at Schmalkald was held on December 22, 1530, at which was laid the foundation of the subsequent Schmalkald League, by which the position of the Reformation to the affairs of the state was more definitely determined. This league was one of the results of the severe and minatory decree of the Diet of November 19, 1530. When, sixteen years later, immediately after the death of Luther, the so-called *Schmalkald War* broke out, the elector John Frederick of Saxony and the landgrave Philip of Hesse, together with their associates of the league, could console their consciences with what Luther had written to Wenceslaus Link from Coburg on September 30, 1530: "They have the Confession, they have the gospel. If they wish, they can accept it; if not, they can leave it alone. *If a war ensues, it will come out of that; and let it come: we have prayed and done enough.*"

As in the course of time everything changes, so the theatre of Luther's activity and life in Coburg has also submitted to the dominion of change. "The little clump of trees, which is called the grove," and in which the daws and ravens held their council under Luther's window, has for a long time been exterminated. Even the old "Fortress Coburg" has, through the influence of time and art, undergone many essential alterations within and without. "The Luther Chamber" itself has been clothed in the dress of modern times, and the inscriptions with which Luther's hands covered the ancient undecorated walls have long been effaced. But "Luther in Coburg" itself is still the same "momentous event" which it was three hundred and fifty-three years ago, and it will so continue as long as his memory lives. Man himself decays and everything earthly around him waxes old, but true greatness and the fruits of righteousness perpetuate their divine influences to the latest generations.

"LUTHER IN COBURG! Momentous event!" Overflowing source of unshaken moral heroism and of unchanging Christian fidelity, many heart-quickening hours have I spent with thee in spiritual intercourse during the past year! How often in the silent winter nights has the deep-toned knell booming forth from the neighboring church-steeple at midnight roused me from profound contemplation on thy greatness! and always has the summer's earliest morning hour called me back to this sketch of thy glorious career at Coburg. And now thy picture stands before my eyes—not clothed in the garment of romantic art, but in nature's simple reality, although but a feeble reflection of what thou really wert as a living man. Many a lineament of force do I miss in this portrait. Such features must necessarily fail, because the age in which thou didst flourish was of more decided character than ours, which would find it hard to endure such exhibitions of moral power as thou didst show. But, even with this defect in my picture, it still displays thine original and unapproachable greatness. A fervid enthusiasm for Christ the Redeemer and a warm sympathy for all the human race are deeply impressed upon thy countenance. Profound earnestness in the prosecution of the battle for the faith and in all that concerns the warfare of men in this tempest-tossed life, combined most closely with a cheerful Christian temper amid temptation and sorrow, beams from thine eye upon all who look up to thee; upon those noble descendants of the pious forefathers who were thy protectors and patrons; upon all who in the present day in all parts of the world believe the truth as it is set forth in the glorious Confessions of the Church.

Spirit of the Living God, thou who hast also spoken through thy servant Luther, build up thy Church, founded upon the imperishable basis of thy word, higher and higher as a temple of pure and spiritual worship! Consecrate, glorify the whole Christian world, from the palace to the cot, as an assembly who shall be partakers of the inheritance of the saints in light! Preserve thy Church from schism! Promote concord within her borders! Aid all who profess the name of Jesus to secure the assurance and blessings of that faith which is active in works of charity! Thus will Thy kingdom come upon earth. Then there will be one fold under one Shepherd, and the promise will be fulfilled, "Fear not, little flock; for it is the Father's good pleasure to give you the kingdom." May that God grant this who is a strong tower and secure refuge for all believers all the world over and in all generations!

THE END.

www.ingramcontent.com/pod-product-compliance
Lightning Source LLC
Chambersburg PA
CBHW031746230426
43669CB00007B/502